S0-AAM-705

#7⁰⁰
DB
1ST

86827231

THOMAS D. LEAHY
NANCY B. LEAHY
3204 VERSAILLE CT.
THOUSAND OAKS, CA 91362

ALSO BY LEE TREVINO

Groove Your Golfing My Way

BOOKS BY SAM BLAIR

Dallas Cowboys: Pro or Con?

First Down, Lifetime to Go

I Believe

Earl Campbell: The Driving Force

They Call Me
SUPER MEX

They Call Me
SUPER MEX

LEE TREVINO
and
Sam Blair

Random House New York

Copyright © 1982 by Lee Trevino Enterprises, Inc.,
and Sam Blair

All rights reserved under International and
Pan-American Copyright Conventions. Published in the
United States by Random House, Inc., New York, and
simultaneously in Canada by Random House of
Canada Limited, Toronto.

Library of Congress Cataloging in Publication Data
Trevino, Lee.
They call me Super Mex.
I. Trevino, Lee. 2. Golfers—United States—Biography.
I. Blair, Sam, 1932– .   II. Title.
GV964.T73A37 1982   796.352′092′4 [B]   82-15677
ISBN 0-394-52336-9

Manufactured in the United States of America
98765432
First Edition

TO CLAUDIA,

who encouraged me when I needed it,

and who not only loves me

but is my best friend

-L. T.

TO KAREN,

who always cares,

always shares

and always believes

-S. B.

Contents

Foreword

Two days before Christmas I stopped by Lee Trevino's house with my two young sons, figuring it was a good time to (1) offer our season's greetings, (2) welcome him home and (3) wish him a good trip. He had just returned from the Panama Open and was leaving again on Christmas Day for Johannesburg and from there to Bophuthatswana, where he would play in golf's first million-dollar tournament.

Talking to Lee can be like that. You catch him coming and going. But on this particular afternoon he planned to stay in one place awhile. His practice was finished for the day and he was busy in the kitchen. He had a large pot of freshly made stew bubbling on the stove for his family's dinner and now he was stacking chairs and stools, getting ready to mop the floor.

Maybe this isn't how you'd expect your typical world-famous golfer to spend a little leisure time at home, but Lee Trevino never has been typical. As his old friend Arnold Salinas likes to say, "Lee would make someone a wonderful wife."

But Lee can be a lot of things. He's a good fisherman, a fine mechanic, an expert yard man and not a bad machine-gunner. Once he even proved to be a dandy lightning rod. Still, he's best at being Lee Trevino, and golf history is richer because he is.

Oh, there are a few things Lee has missed in life. "My frustrated ambition is to play the guitar," he says, and he laughs. "My wife says I'm too fat and my arms are too short to play it worth a damn."

He compensates occasionally by throwing a party and inviting big-league guitarists like Charley Pride and Tom Watson, who picks almost as well as he putts.

Lee will be remembered for his unique climb to the top of his sport, a golfer who captured the world as much with his personality as he did with his game. He comes across as fresh and quick, and he is.

One day we drove to Tenison Park, the East Dallas municipal course that he helped make famous. Lee hadn't visited Tenison in five years and the old-timers glowed when he walked into the clubhouse. He went around shaking hands and laughing, then sat down at a table to drink coffee with some of his old pals. He noticed that one of them, a fellow of sixty-five or so, was wearing three gold necklaces. Lee reached over and held them up.

"Your wife die?" he asked.

When Lee said he wanted me to collaborate on his autobiography I knew it would be a lot of work—and a lot of fun. He was always candid and talkative whenever we met. Usually we sat in his breakfast room, drinking orange juice and coffee, but one day he told me some great stuff in his front driveway while he taught his son Tony how to flush the radiator of his 1949 Ford pickup and fill it with antifreeze.

We also had some good sessions at the British Open. The final day at Royal St. George's was particularly memorable. Lee walked along an old road from the 18th green surrounded by fans. He showed great coordination and agility as he edged toward the clubhouse . . . reaching, signing, handing books and pens back over his shoulder as he accepted more. He was a prime candidate for a busted ankle but he never fell. Finally, he reached the quiet of the locker room, sagged on a bench and whistled.

"Hell, that's like playing rugby," he said. And he knew it wasn't over yet.

He changed shoes, tipped the elderly clubhouse men and teased them about spending all their money on their girl friends. Then he stepped outside into the mob of fans around his car.

He was able to slip into the back seat but found a woman, expensively dressed and well-endowed, leaning through the door. Speaking Spanish with a British accent, she pleaded with him to sign the book for her fifteen-year-old son. Lee grinned and signed one more time.

The car pulled away and the woman clutched the book, beaming.

"I haven't seen anything so thrilling," she exclaimed, "since I was a girl chasing the Beatles!"

I congratulated her on her persistence and good fortune. She heard my accent and smiled. "Do you know Mr. Trevino?" she asked.

I said I did, explaining that I was a journalist from Dallas.

"Well, then you must sign my son's book, too," she said.

As I signed, a dozen youngsters surrounded me, holding their books up for my autograph. Hey, this was all right. Then another boy rushed up and asked, "Who is he?"

"He's from Dallas," someone explained.

The kid looked at me curiously.

"Do you know Jay Ahr?" he asked.

Funny, but he just missed seeing a *real* Dallas star, a guy certainly more memorable than the villainous J. R. Ewing of television's *Dallas*. Long after that melodrama has vanished from the screen, Lee will remain one of the town's rarest products. In fact, in a city intent on blowing up lovely old buildings and putting glass-wrap skyscrapers in their place, he is one of the few remaining landmarks.

But he belongs to the world, not just Dallas or Texas. Lee has touched people everywhere with his heart as well as his humor. Cancer research, children's hospitals, orphanages and golf scholarship programs have benefited from his generosity. He's a guy who drove fifty miles after a round at the Tournament of Champions in response to a spontaneous request that he do a benefit for disabled veterans. He's a guy who played an exhibition in Mississippi to raise money for a pro whose shop burned down. He believes he's fortunate to have lived the life he has and he likes to share it with those in need.

Personally, he gave me everything I needed to write this book. There's just one more thing I want.

His recipe for that stew.

— SAM BLAIR
April 1982

They Call Me
SUPER
MEX

I'm just like a duck. I get up in a new
world every day. Whatever happens
is meant to happen—unless you walk down
the middle of the freeway and wait to
get hit by a truck.

—LEE TREVINO

1.
Alive
and Laughing

The rain didn't look like it would last long that afternoon at the Western Open so Jerry Heard and I decided we'd just relax on the 13th green and have a little picnic. I sent my caddie for soft drinks and hot dogs and we sat on the edge of the green by a lake, me leaning up against my bag and Jerry beside me with his umbrella between his legs.

Then there was a thunderous crack like cannonfire and suddenly I was lifted a foot and a half off the ground. There was a loud, steady ringing in my ears like a tuning fork, my hands were flailing and I couldn't breathe. I was stretched out like a vibrator.

Damn, I thought to myself, this is a helluva penalty for slow play.

Then I fell back on the ground and blacked out.

They say your whole life passes before you at that moment and, believe me, it does. Hey, I never knew I was so bad! I saw a lot of old girl friends. Really, it was like a motion picture going by. I saw my mother, my grandfather, my kids, my wife. I felt no pain. It was a very warm feeling, very satisfying.

Then the reality of being struck by lightning set in. I felt like I wasn't going to pull out of it and one thought crossed my mind: Who would take care of my family?

Until that moment—June 27, 1975—I never had been scared of lightning on a golf course. When I was a little kid I used to practice in the rain a lot. It would be thundering and lightning and I'd just keep hitting golf balls. Even when a kid I knew, the younger brother of actress Dorothy Malone, was killed by lightning on the tee at Dallas Athletic Club in the summer of 1954 it never occurred to me I should be more careful out there.

Lightning was something I always joked about. Just the week before that Western Open at Butler National Golf Club I was paired with Tom Watson in the U.S. Open at Medinah, another course near Chicago, and lightning started crackling just as we went to the first tee. Tom ran back in the clubhouse but I stayed out on the tee and entertained the gallery.

"I'm not scared of lightning," I told them. "I've made my peace with the Lord and he promised he wouldn't throw any darts at me."

You can see how smart I was. Now I was an almost lifeless body on the soggy 13th green and I could see the next morning's headline: SUPER MEX BECOMES SUPER EX.

When I came to, I was lying on my back with my left arm twisted underneath me. People were holding a towel over my face to keep the rain off. I was breathing hard, and from what I remembered from my first aid training in the Marines, I thought my shoulder was broken because I had no feeling in my left side. "Call an ambulance," I said, "and tell them to bring a straight board like they use for people with broken backs."

Jerry Heard was standing a few feet away. He was shaken, but the lightning didn't catch him like it did me. I had four burn spots on my left shoulder where the lightning came out of my body. Evidently that bolt skipped off the lake, shot through the metal shafts in my bag and came up my back.

Crazy things happened elsewhere on the course. Lightning knocked a club out of Bobby Nichols' hands, but he wasn't seriously hurt. Arnold Palmer felt it, too. It sent his club about 40 yards down the fairway. But it really did a number on me.

By the time we reached the hospital I was scared to death. I was sure the news was all over the country, so I called home to talk to Clyde. That's my wife, Claudia. "How do you feel?" she asked me. "Sensational," I said. "For the first time in my life I was six feet two."

There I was dying and I was making jokes.

The doctor hadn't arrived in the Emergency Room yet. I was stretched out on my stomach with ice packs on my back where it had been burned. Jerry was sitting on an examining table next to me. Neither of us had any clothes on; just white sheets covering our bodies.

Jerry felt all right but when that lightning hit his umbrella the fire hit the inside of his thighs and burned off all the pubic hair. The doctor finally walked in. She was a good-looking lady about forty years old. She looked me over, then turned to Jerry and asked, "Now, where did you get burned?" He clutched that sheet and said, "No, no problem. I'm just fine." He wasn't about to pull that sheet back.

I asked the doctor about the numbness in my left side and why I couldn't breathe. "I can't tell you a lot about lightning," she said. "I don't get too many lightning victims in here. They go straight to the morgue."

That was encouraging.

"You're one of the few to get hit and survive it," she told me. "The electrical shock stops the heartbeat, but the blood is still rushing and it takes very little for your heart to rupture. That kills you immediately."

She explained that the symptoms I had, with the numbness in my left side, were like having a heart attack. I had blood in my urine and she said I should spend some time in the Intensive Care Unit where they could watch me closely. Jerry stayed overnight, then went back to Butler and finished the tournament. Me, I spent the weekend in ICU.

It's never dark in that room. There were a lot of patients in beds in sort of a circular arrangement with nurses in the middle where they can observe everyone. Each patient is hooked up to a machine and all you hear is beep . . . beep . . . beep. You know if you don't hear one of those beeps that someone's heart has stopped.

They gave me pills to make me sleep, but the more I thought about everything the more determined I was to stay awake. So for two days and two nights I lay there, with all those wires on me, listening to that monitor of my heartbeat and thinking what could happen. My accident had been like a child cutting himself. At that particular moment it doesn't scare you. It's always afterward, when you realize what could have happened, that you feel afraid.

Beep . . . beep . . . beep. Right above the monitor was a big clock with a sweep second hand. I forced myself to stay awake, watching that clock. With each sweep of that hand, I knew I had lived another minute.

I could barely walk when I left the hospital and got on a plane to fly home to El Paso. The electrical shock tore up all the muscle tone in my body and I didn't know what to expect. I kept taking stress tests to learn if my heart was damaged in any way but I checked out fine. In a few days I was feeling much better, so I went out and started hitting golf balls. A couple of weeks later I headed for the British Open at Carnoustie in Scotland. I didn't play well, but I was just delighted to be there, alive and laughing.

My nerves weren't too good. I was playing in Worcester, Massachusetts, and the clouds were kind of boiling and I heard thunder in the distance. Just then a lady took a picture of me with a flash camera and I jumped about ten feet in the air. For a while, I got cold chills and goosebumps all over my body when I saw lightning. Once, in Hartford, we were riding into the hotel and it was raining. Then it started lightning bad—like flicking the lights on and off in a dark room. So I ducked my head below the car's dashboard where I couldn't see it and covered my eyes.

Physically, I had more problems than I first realized.

The electrical shock dissolved the lubricant between the discs in my vertebrae, and that would mean trouble on down the line. Vertebrae are like wheel bearings of your car packed in grease. If the grease is gone, you're going to wear the bearings out. That's what was happening to the disc in my lower back. Sooner or later I would put too much strain on it and I would be in trouble.

In May of 1976, a couple of weeks after I won the Colonial tournament in Fort Worth, I was at home and my wife asked me to lift a large potted plant so she could put a protective metal sheet between it and the carpet. I picked it up and my back snapped. It sounded like a knuckle popping. An electrical sensation ran up and down my legs and back. I was frozen in that bent-over position for about ten seconds, then I straightened up, wondering what had happened to my back. I had no idea then how bad it was.

I played in Hartford and finished fourth, but my back hurt so much that I went to an osteopath every morning just to get manipulated and get the pressure off it. It kept getting worse, so I withdrew from the U.S. and British Opens that summer, hoping it would improve. Nothing helped. By November my back was so bad that I whiffed a tee shot at a tournament in Mexico. I still finished second by one shot but I had to finish the tournament in a golf cart, hitting the ball along the ground. I could only stand for about two minutes at a time. I was in such misery I wanted somebody to shoot me.

I called the Mayo Clinic, but they told me there was no point in my going all the way to Rochester, Minnesota, when there were some fine neurosurgeons nearer by in Houston. So through Charlie Crowder, a friend who owns the Santa Teresa development in New Mexico, I was introduced to Dr. Antonio Moure, a Spaniard who practices at Park Plaza Hospital.

Dr. Moure ran tests on me for four or five days and then, by injecting dye in my spinal cord, he located my trouble— a ruptured disc between the fourth and fifth vertebrae. He said he needed to operate and remove it.

"Doc," I said, "will I ever be able to play golf again?"

"Oh," he said, "you'll be better than ever."

"Well, Doc, your reputation's on the line," I told him. "If you're not successful, you'll be using all those knives in the kitchen."

But I took his word on it and went ahead with the surgery. Then I found out he had never played golf!

I was in tremendous pain. Clyde knows how bad it was because she had a bed moved into my room and stayed with me for eight days. I don't know how I would have endured that pain if it hadn't been Thanksgiving weekend. I watched a dozen football games on television and bet on all of them. The nurses kept coming in to take my blood pressure during a close game, when I was excited, and they couldn't get an accurate reading. They got pretty frustrated with me.

They got even, though, waking me up in the middle of the night to give me a sleeping pill. I'd say, "Hey, I'm sleeping. Why do I want a sleeping pill now?"

When it was time to go to therapy in the next building each day, Macho Lee refused to be pushed in a wheelchair. I insisted on walking, but I had such pain in my legs I had to lie down in the elevator. When the doors opened, some people tried to step in and saw me stretched out. "Don't worry about it, folks," I said, "I'm just resting for a minute."

I worked extremely hard in therapy, but just stretching hurt bad. I had no strength in my back and I had tears in my eyes when I did those exercises. The therapy room staff was composed of about six or seven young women; they made it a fun place, even if they treated all the patients like children. I'd strain like mad to barely lift my leg off the floor and they'd exclaim, "Ooh, that's wonderful! Man, that is great!"

And I'd say, "Sonuvabitch! I can't get this thing more than four inches off the ground."

But when I left the hospital I was convinced I was going to make it back. The only thing I thought about was the challenge of getting in shape, returning to the tour, playing well again, and winning. I was in extreme pain for two years and I needed pills. Sometimes during a long plane flight I had muscle spasms so bad I couldn't get out of my seat when we landed. But in July of 1977, eight months after my surgery, I won the Canadian Open. I was on my way again.

That was the most satisfying victory of my career and it ended one tough week. We played in Toronto at Glen Abbey, the course Jack Nicklaus redesigned, and with the greens curled around like horseshoes, it's extremely difficult. You had to be absolutely perfect with your iron shots. My chipping and putting really won it for me because I still didn't have enough power to hit my drives very far. Back at the hotel I spent a lot of time taking hot baths to relax my muscles and hanging upside down in a gravity machine to stretch my lower back. I played the last round with Jack and won by one shot. He seemed delighted that I did it on his course.

Since then I've won the Tournament Players Championship and the Tournament of Champions, two of the most prestigious on the tour. But there was a victory at Memphis that gave me a special sensation. That one was interrupted by lightning during the final round when I was on the 7th green and not playing well. But I went to the clubhouse and spent an hour thinking about what I was doing wrong. When the sun came out I went back on the course, birdied three of the next four holes and won. Lightning sure didn't ruin my day there.

But I've set several track records getting to cover when lightning started cracking at other tournaments. Once I was way out on the 15th during the Byron Nelson Classic when I heard the siren suspending play. I could have taken Bob Hayes' gold medal coming in. I was in the clubhouse before some of the guys on the 9th green.

I still have problems with my back sometimes. In May of 1981 I had to drop out of competition for about a month because it hurt so much. I went to Houston to see Dr. Moure. He couldn't find anything besides strained ligaments, but he sent me to another specialist for a second opinion. That doctor couldn't find anything major and finally said, "Just to be certain, let me check your prostate."

Clyde was in the examining room with us, but she said, "I believe I'll wait outside."

As the doctor slipped on the rubber glove, he asked me, "You ever done this before?"

I looked back over my shoulder. "I've proposed to two doctors," I said.

There were times I couldn't joke about it, though.

I continued playing erratically through the early months of 1982. Some days my back gave me so much pain that I couldn't bend over to tie my shoes. Finally, I went to Plano, a suburb north of Dallas, and saw Dr. Justo Gonzales. I'd heard he was a good pain doctor and I had one helluva pain.

He gave me a CAT-scan, where I lay down inside a big tube for x-rays, and he discovered one of the main nerves from my spinal cord was pinched. This meant another operation but I was in Plano General Hospital just a couple of days for this one. Dr. Ralph Rashbaum blocked the nerve by burning it with some type of microwave to deaden it. I went home feeling better than I had felt in months.

There also have been special rewards for all that misery. After the publicity about my back trouble, a mattress company hired me to film a commercial. So I realized my life's ambition: to get paid for lying down.

And in 1980 the Golf Writers of America voted me the Ben Hogan Award, which is given to a player who overcomes a serious physical setback. It's named for Hogan because he once almost got wiped out when his car and a bus collided on a highway near El Paso.

I first saw the Ben Hogan trophy at a banquet in New York many years ago and my wife told me, "That's one I really want you to win." "Honey, are you crazy?" I asked her. "I'd have to get run over by a bus!"

Well, I found another way.

Now I sure as hell wouldn't recommend being struck by lightning, but it turned my life around. It made me appreciate everything I had.

Since then I've taken a completely different attitude about the game and about life. I'm more of a family man, spending more time with my wife and kids. Now we go to church together. Before, I felt if I can play golf this good then everyone can stand me, whatever I do. That's not so. There are other things in life that matter.

I knew I was a lucky man and I had no reason to gripe about anything ever again. Now sometimes when I start getting hot about a bad round, poor weather or a screwed-up travel schedule, I tell myself, "You dummy, you could be out picking up range balls right now!"

I got a kick out of beating the odds. Whatever I've done, I've never been afraid to gamble. I think life is a gamble. In everything I do there has to be something at stake, whether it's a dinner, a drink or a golf ball. The challenge has to be there.

Years ago, when I was fresh out of the Marines and working nights at Hardy's Driving Range in Dallas, my old pal Arnold Salinas and I played at Tenison Park most mornings. One day we had a game with four guys, bet $5 a man, and were one down when we reached the 17th tee. Arnold looked real nervous.

While the other guys were hitting, he leaned over to me and asked, "You got any money?"

"No," I said. "Do you?" Hell, we were both broke.

It was time for us to hit. "Well, partner," I told Arnold, "we better play our asses off."

I birdied the last two holes and we won, one up. We grabbed the money, jumped in my ol' Oldsmobile and took off down East Grand to a barbecue stand. We tossed our money on the table, ordered some beer and laughed like crazy.

No matter what the stakes, the sensation of producing under pressure is always there. I hope I never forget what I had to do to make it happen.

2.
Treasure in a Pasture

When my grandfather moved us into that old house in the pasture off Walnut Hill Lane I noticed some people over in what looked like another pasture every day and wondered what they were doing. I had no idea they were playing golf. I always figured you spent your time outdoors farming, fishing, or hunting.

This was in 1947 and I was seven years old. Lee Buck Trevino, country boy, had moved to the big city of Dallas. I didn't know Ben Hogan and Byron Nelson from the Lone Ranger and Tonto. If somebody had asked me, "What is golf ?," I would have wanted to know when the season was and did they fly fast or did you shoot them on the ground.

But here I was, living 100 yards from the 7th fairway at the Dallas Athletic Club course, and after a lot of watching, I did figure out one thing. There was high rough on the right of Number 7. I went over there and started finding golf balls.

One day a guy came over and asked, "Have you got any

balls?" "Yes, sir," I said. He took the five I showed him and handed me a dollar bill. Hey, that excited me.

I told myself, "Maybe I can make some money in this game."

Pretty soon I walked across Coit Road to the clubhouse. I hung around the caddie shed and began to learn about the game. I met Big Mac, the caddie master, and by the time I was eight I was carrying a bag. It was a lot different from the life I knew on the farm but it was fun. And the money I made caddying helped put food on the table. My mother and grandfather needed anything they could get.

I don't know who my father was. I never asked about him, and they never mentioned him. I do know my parents never married. To this day you can check at Parkland Hospital in Dallas and you'll find the record of my birth on December 1, 1939. The name of Juanita Trevino is listed as mother and my name is just there as Lee. So I took my mother's name. She lived with my grandfather, Joe Trevino, a wiry little man with a helluva lot of spirit.

I do have a faint memory of my mother once taking me to visit a man who may have been my father. We lived on a farm then and it was snowing. I don't know how old I was, but I was walking. We walked two or three miles through the snow and ice to this old house. We went in and there was a man propped up in bed.

This gentleman must have injured his back, because there was a chair turned upside down and backward behind his pillows. I'm pretty sure he was my father because I had seen them together other times.

I didn't think that much about not knowing my father when I was a kid. We were busy just trying to exist. Now? Sure, I'd like to know. It doesn't make that much difference, but I am curious.

It's not a sensitive subject with me. My kids know. Everybody knows. Reality is reality. Besides, my grandfather was the best father I could have ever had. He was unbelievable.

When I was very young he was a tenant farmer, working for a man named Tucker who owned some land near Rowlett, a little town north of Garland. Garland is a suburb east of Dallas and a good-sized city now, but then it was just a country town. My grandfather was born in Monterrey, Mexico, but moved to Texas as a young boy, and he worked hard all his life for very little money. He raised cotton and onions, and when he had harvested those crops, Mr. Tucker sent him and my Uncle Lupe out to cut wood in the river bottom. He told them just to stack it and leave it there and he paid them a dollar a cord. He didn't need the wood and he didn't plan to sell it. He was just creating work; giving them a chance to earn money rather than have to take welfare.

By the time I was five I was out in the fields too. I thought hard work was just how life was. I was twenty-one years old before I knew Manual Labor wasn't a Mexican.

When the cotton was ready for harvest in September I pulled a bag through the fields, filling it with bolls. Then we planted onions. God, that was the worst smell in the world! When we had a hailstorm it beat down those onions so much we'd cry for a month.

Earlier than that, when I was just big enough to walk, my grandfather took me out with him, hunting rabbits and crawdad fishing. We'd bring a batch of crawdads in and my mother would serve us fried tails for supper. We thought we were just surviving. Hell, today that's a delicacy. You go to New York and order that and it will cost you an arm and a leg.

We had an old 1929 Model A Ford, a two-seater with a tar top, and one day when we were fishing at Rowlett Creek we were caught in a storm. We jumped in the car, but hailstones tore right through that roof and my grandfather covered me with his body. It's strange, but that's one of the funniest things I remember about him.

It seems even stranger when I remember how I almost killed him.

Because we were so poor we were very conservative in what we used and how we used it. When we went rabbit hunting my grandfather took his 16-gauge shotgun, but we always carried a .22 rifle, too. If we saw a rabbit sitting, he would hand me the shotgun and shoot the rabbit with the .22, simply because the .22 shell was much cheaper. Well, once I was walking behind him on a trail, carrying the .22. I figured the safety was on and there was no shell in the chamber, so I thought, just for a joke, I'd aim the gun at him and pull the trigger.

I raised the gun but then something told me not to do it. So I pointed the gun at the ground, pulled the trigger and it fired. That was the damnedest thing in the world and it taught me a tremendous lesson.

My mother did marry while we lived on that farm. The man's name was Barrett, but he didn't stay long. One day he just took off to Dallas and didn't come back. She never got a divorce—I don't believe she ever really counted on seeing him again. He was just another wanderer. Some men are like that. A few years ago I was visiting with a woman in a store on Greenville Avenue and she told me how her husband left one day to get a loaf of bread and didn't come back for twenty-five years. Then one day he walked in the house. I wonder if he had the bread?

When I wasn't working in the fields or hunting or fishing, I could be the meanest little cuss in the world. One day, when I was five, my little sister Anna and I built a fire outside. I threw a can in the fire, then told her, "Give me that can." She reached in to grab it and burned her whole hand.

They beat me so hard that I ran through a corn patch and hid. I was afraid to come home, so finally my Uncle Lupe came out and found me.

Some good friends, the Valle family, visited us one Sunday and I was really excited because there was a boy, Johnny, about my age. We had an old Jersey cow with a couple of horns on her and I wanted to impress Johnny's little sister.

"Watch this cow chase me!" I yelled, and climbed over the fence and into the pen. I taunted her and here she came. I laughed and ran for the fence. Then I hit the top board and the damn thing broke. I fell back in and that cow was almost on me. My sister Josephine dragged me under the fence just in time. That old cow almost stomped me to death, but once I got outside, oh, it was funny.

Joe Valle worked in Dallas and he told my grandfather there were jobs open at Hillcrest Cemetery. Soon we were packing up to leave the Tucker farm. My grandfather was going to work as a gravedigger. The pay wasn't much. When he retired years later he still wasn't making over $40 a week. But the work was steady and there was a house included.

My grandfather loaded all of our things into one of those big wooden trailers you haul cotton in; it had a long wagon tongue that he tied to the back of our car. We piled into that Model A Ford and clattered away from the farm. My sisters and I sat in the back seat, excited about going to the big city.

We passed through Garland and headed for Dallas on Forest Lane. Well, here came a guy driving pretty fast toward the intersection at Greenville Avenue. He looked like he was two hundred yards away, though, and my grandfather figured we could make it through the intersection. He was wrong.

That guy threw on his brakes but he couldn't stop in time. His car came right between our car and the trailer, just knocked that ol' wagon tongue off clean. Nobody was hurt and nothing was damaged, but my grandfather had to work until dark getting that trailer hitched to the car again. My sisters and I thought it was fun. We got out and chased rabbits in a cotton field.

I'll never forget going to that old, unpainted house. Really, it was just a four-room shack with some cottonwood trees and a lake out front. No plumbing, no electricity, no windows, no wallpaper. One room, which turned out to be the kitchen, had a dirt floor. The shack was sitting there surrounded by sunflowers and Johnson grass six feet high with cattle roaming about. It was ugly, but it was something new. It was home.

We lived north of Northwest Highway and there wasn't much nearby. The cemetery was a mile south, and there were a couple of houses on Hillcrest about a mile west. Then there was DAC Country Club, which became Glen Lakes Country Club a few years later when DAC moved to a new location. Today this is the heart of booming North Dallas. North Park shopping center sprawls across the land where I hunted rabbits and there are high-rise office buildings in all directions. The golf course where I learned to play is gone and so is our shack. Now it's Glen Lakes Estates. Mary Kay Ash, the woman who made a fortune in the cosmetics business, has a beautiful home where our house stood. The lake and the cottonwoods are still there, though.

Our lifestyle was pretty primitive.

We used lake water to wash clothes and for baths. Twice a week we heated water on an old pot-bellied, wood-burning stove and filled a big Number 3 metal tub. My sisters and I bathed in it, all of us using the same water. The grownups weren't going to heat water for each of us.

My grandfather hauled drinking water home from the cemetery in five-gallon milk cans, and we used that for all our cooking. There were no cabinets in the kitchen, and for a closet we hammered a nail into the wall. It wasn't much but it was enough. We still could hang up all our clothes.

My Uncle Lupe lived with us and he had his own room. The rest of us slept in one room, my grandfather using our only real mattress. On cold nights my mother and us kids would sleep together in one bed on old canvas sacks stuffed with dry grass. We put a huge log in the stove that would burn half the night. Then someone got up in the freezing cold to start another fire. But when the stove fired up, that baby got so hot it would turn red. I used to joke that Mexicans are so dark from sleeping next to those stoves. We would warm the front side, then rotate and warm the back side. We're barbecued!

We had a cow, a Holstein named Katie, and I had to milk her every night. Once a year we used to take her and breed her with a bull, bring her home, have her calved, then sell the calf. We had a big garden and we raised hogs. I hated to feel the first frost hit because that meant hog-killing time. That was a mess, but one hog provided our meat and sausage for a year. And the gristly meat in his head made great tamales.

That little lake was full of fish. I caught so many for our dinners that I called it Lake Safeway. Once there was a big seven-pound bass looking at me from the edge of the lake, where the water was down so low that part of his back was exposed. Every time I'd move close to him he went to deeper water. Then when I moved back he'd come out. I couldn't figure how to get him, so I went to the house, got my grandfather's shotgun, shot the damn thing and pulled him out of the water.

We bought only flour, sugar, salt and pepper at the store. Everything else we raised or brought in from hunting and fishing. All our food was fried in lard made from hog fat, which was bad for our diet but was the only way we could do it. We couldn't afford to buy peanut or vegetable oil. And we sure couldn't afford any treats.

One day, years later, Tom Watson and I were talking. I laughed real big. He could see my teeth and was surprised I didn't have any fillings. I told him, "You don't get cavities when you're raised on beans."

I never had candy as a kid. Sugar cane was about the sweetest thing we ever got, or some sugar sprinkled on a biscuit. But I know kids love candy. In 1968, after I won the U.S. Open, I went to the PGA championship in San Antonio and gave a clinic for about four thousand underprivileged kids in a park. Dr Pepper gave everyone free drinks and I bought them candy—$1,200 worth.

Now when I take my family to Mazatlán on vacation I always drive my kids through the slums to show them how some people have to live. It's no different from how I had it as a kid, except we were sitting out in that pasture by ourselves.

I was skinny as a rail when I was eight, but I still got into the action at the club, caddying for members and playing golf and cards with all the black caddies who rode out to the course on the old streetcars that ran across Dallas then. That's where I learned my killer instinct, playing games with those black caddies and betting everything I had earned that day. I learned courage from my grandfather in the graveyard at night.

As soon as we moved into that shack I started walking a mile over to the cemetery to take him his lunch. I would find him working alone, sometimes so deep in the ground I couldn't see his head until I looked into the black, muddy hole. He dug it the hard way, with pick and shovel, and he was very proud of his work. With him it was an art, digging a grave seven feet long, six feet deep and three feet wide with sides as smooth as silk.

On summer nights he'd take me with him to the cemetery to move the water hoses and sprinklers. It was pitch dark but he knew exactly where everything was.

He told me, "Take this sprinkler and move it fifty feet over there." I was shaking but I knew I had to do it. "Lee," he said, "you're gonna hear some noises but don't worry. That's just your footsteps echoing off the gravestones." Well, it was just like he said, and pretty soon I was going all over the cemetery. I wasn't afraid any more.

My grandfather wasn't more than five feet four inches tall and one hundred and thirty-five pounds, but he worked like hell and loved to drink beer in those joints along Greenville Avenue on Friday and Saturday nights. He loved to fight, too, although he was too little to whip anybody. That didn't stop him, though. I still laugh when I remember him coming home all cut up. He was still proud. Nobody ever whipped his spirit.

My mother was a heavy woman. She probably weighed one hundred and sixty-five pounds but was only five two. She was an extremely hard worker, but like my grandfather, she couldn't read or write. When people around North Dallas found out she would do day work they would drive by and pick her up and she'd go clean their houses. That really was the only communication she had with the outside world. She was more or less a prisoner living out there in our shack. She had no place else to go.

There wasn't much fun in our lives, but she was a happy lady. I guess I got some of my traits from her. She was loud, talked a lot, made a joke out of everything. She started calling me Buck when I was a little kid, so I took it for a middle name. On wash days she'd put our clothes in an old black pot over an outdoor fire, then scrub them on a rubboard, singing and giggling.

The Caruth family had owned all the land for miles around since 1852. W. W. Caruth, who lived with his wife on the old family estate between Northwest Highway and Southwestern Boulevard, provided houses for some of the cemetery workers, and he loved to come by our place to hunt doves and to fish. He and I became good friends, sitting out by the lake and walking through the fields hunting doves. He'd shoot them and I'd run them down for him.

He was pretty old then, a short, heavy man, but he still liked to play golf. He was one of the first DAC members I caddied for. Some of my other early bags were Henry Klepak, an attorney; Tex Cole, who owned some liquor stores; and Tony Bifano, whose family had Bifano's Furs downtown and a swell restaurant in Highland Park called Bali Hai. The caddie fee was sixty-five cents for nine holes or $1.25 for eighteen, but sometimes I was lucky and got a big tip.

Tony Bifano was a good player, and once when he had a really hot round he gave me a $10 bill. I thought I was the richest kid in the world! I couldn't wait to get home, to show it off. That made living easier for a while.

DAC was one of the top clubs in town. Graham Ross was the pro and Dick Carter the assistant and they had a lot of players out there. Big Mac, the caddie master, often had as many as one hundred and thirty caddies working on Saturday. I caddied primarily for the same men all the time. They seemed to like me. I was a good caddie, a hustling kid who didn't mind the work. If they wanted to hit balls late, I went out and chased them until dark.

Only one player ever fired me. I was working for a different man that day and we had just crossed Coit Road and reached Number 5, a par-5 that paralleled Walnut Hill Lane. It was a hot day and two groups were waiting at the tee, so my man went over to the little concession stand and drank about five beers. I mean he inhaled 'em! Then his turn finally came on the tee.

Well, he took a 4-wood and made the mightiest swing I've ever seen. He hit about five inches behind the ball and the divot flipped up on the ball and covered it. He looked up and wondered where he had hit the ball. He looked at me and said, "Where did the ball go? Where did the ball go?" But I couldn't answer him. I was on the ground, laughing.

I couldn't get up, so I crawled over and pulled the divot back and showed him his ball. He was so mad he fired me on the spot. He called over another caddie to carry double and I took off as soon as I could stand up.

I have a lot of great memories about that course. That's where I started my game. I caddied for one little old man real late on Sundays, and as soon as we got out of sight from the clubhouse he'd let me play him for my caddie fee, double or nothing. I beat him every time.

I learned to play well and practice hard. I played my ass off, because I wanted to beat the other caddies. We had three holes behind the caddie shed—one about 100 yards, another about 125, another about 60. We'd find some old clubs and start hitting. We had as many as sixteen guys playing for quarters. I'd hit a shot and throw the club 50 yards to another guy where he could hit. As soon as he'd hit, he'd throw the club to another guy. It might take thirty minutes to play one 100-yard hole with clubs flying around like that but it was great experience. It sharpened my game and my competitive spirit.

From playing in back of the caddie shed to winning the U.S. and British Opens was a helluva long trip but I made it, and I never had a lesson. Jack Grout taught Nicklaus how to play. Stan Thirsk taught Watson how to play. *I* taught me how to play.

As a person, I changed a lot because of my exposure to those caddies. I went from a country kid to a cool kitty from the city. I was smoking when I was ten, something I picked up from older caddies, just like the foul language. I was a little boy thrown in with men. Some of them were dangerous people who carried knives and guns. Hardly a day passed that I didn't watch a knife fight. We were shooting dice and playing cards and there always were arguments.

It was an education of hard knocks. I'm not saying it's what all kids should do; I was just thrown into it. I was polite to adults, but when I wasn't around them I was rowdy. I had no supervision. I stayed out late. I was pretty much on my own from the time I was eight.

But there were special times I enjoy remembering.

Some young caddies came from South Dallas on Saturday morning, and rather than have them go all the way home that night, I'd bring them to my house. We'd go to the store and buy baloney, wieners, bread and mustard, I'd get some blankets and we'd camp out by the lake. We'd eat and fish, then go to sleep. Next morning we woke up early and walked back over to the clubhouse to caddie again.

And we had some good family gatherings on Sunday afternoons when everyone visited and played games. It's something we don't have now as much. I guess television has taken a lot away from people. We didn't have television then, or money to do anything else. My Uncle Joe had two boys a little younger than me and he'd bring his family in from Garland. The Valle family had moved into a house nearby and they walked over to our place. We'd play football with beer cans or ride bicycles or go swimming in the lake.

We lived in the Vickery community, and whenever I went to school I attended Vickery School on the other side of Greenville Avenue beyond the country club. I usually skipped school two or three days a week. It was so damn easy. We had no phone, so the truant officer couldn't call. Coming by to see my mother at our house out in the middle of nowhere wasn't easy, particularly since the gate was locked. And she had no education, so she had no feel for school. I just did what I wanted to do.

I wasn't dumb. My teachers said I'd be amazed how well I could do if I came every day. Well, once I went to school for two solid weeks and they were right!

My grandfather cut the lawn for a little lady named Mrs. Peters, and when her husband died of a heart attack I spent two weeks with her. She gave me his bed, one of those where you can elevate the head or feet, and a pillow and mattress. She gave me his .22 rifle, too, and for the first time I had the luxury of sitting on indoor plumbing. Man, I thought I was in high cotton! But she also gave me discipline. I was in school every day and she would not tolerate my not doing my homework.

She made me bring all my books home. She gave me spelling tests and I learned every word. In school, I made one hundred on every test and I was proud of it. But as soon as I left I went back to my old ways. Today, I feel much differently about education. I will not tolerate my children missing school and not getting an excellent education. But then my mind was somewhere else.

I was the best athlete in school. Football, soccer, softball . . . I was a star. I had most of my height by the time I was fourteen but I wasn't heavy. I could move and I always was fast with my mind. The coaches from Hillcrest High School came to see me play, anxious for the day I got there. I never did.

When I was eleven, the Civitans organized the first kids' baseball league in our area and I played on a swell little team, the Dixie Cream Doughnut Kings. There were two brothers on my team, Tom and Gene Hunt, and their mother, Mrs. Virginia Hunt, always drove by our pasture gate on Walnut Hill Lane and took me along to games and practices in their 1947 Hudson.

I played catcher most of the time, but if the game was going badly, I'd go out to the mound, hand the pitcher my chest protector and mask and tell him, "Look, you get behind the plate. I'll pitch."

We had a good record, but we never could beat the team from Reed's Orphanage. Those orphans had a great farm system. They grew up playing together on a big farm where Presbyterian Hospital now stands.

We played baseball at Vickery Park, a wonderful place for kids. It had a miniature golf course, an archery range, all sorts of amusement rides and refreshment stands. I loved to go there on a hot summer day and eat a snowcone.

Vickery Park also had the greatest pool in town; but I couldn't swim there. If you were dark-skinned you couldn't get in. Now someone would take them to court tomorrow for that, but then it was up to the guy selling tickets at the gate to decide who came in. If you looked too dark to him, you didn't swim at Vickery Park.

I didn't know Arnold and Albert Salinas, who work for me now in Lee Trevino Enterprises, but they knew about the rule, too. Arnold never could buy a ticket but Albert could because he is light-complexioned. When Albert got inside, he'd make funny faces at Arnold through the fence.

It didn't bother me, though, because I liked to skinny-dip with the orphanage kids in a pond. That water was cold as ice, and we screamed and splashed around in our birthday suits. We didn't give a damn about that swimming pool.

There was no discrimination otherwise. I went roller skating a lot at Deuback's rink, farther out Greenville across the road from where Royal Oaks Country Club is now. I ate hamburgers at Pete's, a little bitty place in Vickery Square where I could drink beer even when I was a kid; and at the Green Top Grill, a drive-in down Greenville with a great carhop named Ma. If I was broke, she'd let me pay her later. For movies, we went farther down Greenville to the Granada, which was fairly new; and the Arcadia, which was older but still a first-class neighborhood theater. Now the Arcadia shows Spanish-language films, which would have left me cold in those days.

We never spoke Spanish in my home when I was a kid and I barely knew the language until I moved to El Paso in 1966. The first time I drove into Mexico, the officer at the border asked me in Spanish how many cylinders my car had. I thought he asked me how many children. "Uno," I said. His eyes got real wide and he exclaimed, "Uno?" He thought I had a motorcycle under the hood.

But my favorite hangout was Hardy's Driving Range. It was a couple of miles from my house, on Lovers Lane near Greenville, and I first went there one night to hit golf balls when I was eight. I was barefoot and wearing some old tattered jeans and a T-shirt. I went with Jack Shawver, whose dad was greens superintendent at DAC. Jack was a real tall kid about four years older than me. He had played golf all his life and he couldn't understand why he never could beat me.

Well, my arms weren't much bigger than the club shafts

but I could knock the hell out of the ball. Hardy Greenwood, who owned the range, watched me hit balls that night and he never forgot. Every once in a while through the years Hardy would ask about me and what I was doing, like he had a special interest in me. I sure had a special interest in his driving range. I would have gone there and hit balls in the middle of the night if I could.

I quit school when I was fourteen, before I entered the eighth grade. There was no hassle. I was tired of school and my mother thought I was old enough to take a full-time job. The truant officer told her it was necessary to go before a judge and get a work permit because of my age. She did, and I was free to go to work. It was easy. Too damn easy.

Louis Shawver still was greens superintendent at the country club, but now it was called Glen Lakes. He hired me to work on his crew. It was 1954 and I earned $1,250 that year. I still have the W-2 form.

My mother and I weren't real close when I was growing up because all of us were struggling to exist and I was gone so much, working and playing golf. If I had it to do over, I believe I'd spend more time with her.

But we had some great times after I started winning a lot of money in golf. After my first U.S. Open championship I bought her a house north of Royal Oaks Country Club, had it redecorated and filled with new furniture. I wouldn't let her see it until it was finished, and then I told her, "Throw away everything old. I'm moving you into a new house."

She didn't want to leave and neither did my grandfather, although for about three years they had rented an old house that was almost condemned. Still, it was the first place where she ever had the luxury of electricity and running water, and she liked it. My grandfather didn't want to leave his garden there.

But when she saw the new house she was thrilled. She said, "Who would want anything old in a house this gorgeous?"

I told the interior decorator, "You take all the old junk." Ten years later I concluded that the furniture she threw out was worth five times as much as the new because it was all antique—brass beds, Victrolas, chests of drawers, foot lockers, stuff they'd used for many, many years.

Mother was quite happy there, especially after I showed her how to dial the telephone. My grandfather was, too, once he chopped out all the hedges in the back yard and planted a garden. But he only lived there a few months. He died in that house early in 1969 when he was eighty. He lived long enough to see me make it big in golf, though, and that pleased him.

In the summer of 1968, Clyde and I had come back to Dallas to visit after I won the U.S. Open. We found my grandfather sitting in Potsy's Barbecue Grill on Greenville Avenue, drinking beer. "Hey, let me buy some," I told him, and I put a $100 bill on the bar. He looked at that money and gave me a helluva smile.

When we left, I told the lady tending bar, "Don't ever let him pay for another beer. Just keep his tab and I'll come by every two or three months and pay you." That was one of the greatest pleasures I ever had.

My grandfather loved the goldfish in the pond near the front gate at Hillcrest Cemetery. He used to feed those goldfish all the time. His wife was buried in Rowlett, but he told me he wanted to be buried by that pond. He got his wish.

In October of 1971 my mother was buried beside him. She died of cancer at the age of forty-eight. She had followed my golf closely the last couple of years and was quite happy with my success. When I beat Jack Nicklaus in a playoff to win the U.S. Open in June of 1971, she was very sick but she watched me on television. She told the *Dallas Morning News,* "I'm really proud of that boy."

I still live near the cemetery and I'm glad. Every once in a while I go by, sit by their graves and talk to them.

I just tell them everything is all right.

3.
Home on the Range

My junior golf career began and ended when I was fifteen and entered the *Dallas Times Herald* tournament.

I qualified with a 77 at Stevens Park, the municipal course in the Oak Cliff section of Dallas. Strange as it may seem, that was the first complete round of golf I'd ever played. I had hit nine billion balls by then and played a lot of competitive golf with money on the line, but that always was as a caddie, sneaking in a few holes out of sight of the clubhouse or on that little layout behind the caddie shed at Glen Lakes. This time I was in official match play, trying to win the championship of the fifteen-year-old division. It was good experience, even if it didn't last long.

In the first round I drew a left-hander whose name I can't remember and beat him pretty badly. The second round I drew a black player named Frankie Galloway. This was 1955 and it may have surprised a lot of people that a black kid was playing in a big tournament like this in the South. I didn't think anything about that, but it sure impressed me on the first tee to see Frankie Galloway had a mustache, goatee and sideburns.

This kid's fifteen years old? I said to myself. The rest of us still had pimples and hadn't even started shaving yet and he was all ready. He had a lot of knowledge about the game, too. I hit the ball awfully long but he hit it nine miles. He was big and he could play. He knocked me out on 17 and won, 2 and 1, but he didn't win the title. The Teter brothers dominated junior golf in Dallas then. Ross won the fifteen-year-old division and Gene won the sixteen-year-old. I never heard of Frankie Galloway again.

That was the extent of my amateur career except for some competition in the Marine Corps a few years later. I only played in the *Times Herald* tournament because Hardy Greenwood entered me and furnished me a complete set of clubs and a pair of golf shoes. I was working full-time at Hardy's Driving Range then and I loved golf, but I didn't think I could ever play well enough to have a career. Hardy saw a future for me in golf before I did.

After I quit school and worked at Glen Lakes a few months, he sent his handy man, Norman Scott, by my house and asked me to come see him at the range. Hardy asked me if I wanted to work for him. "Doing what?" I asked. "Picking up balls at the range," he said. I guess I didn't act real eager so Hardy said, "Are you going to mow greens and fairways all your life, or do you want to be a golfer? I've never forgotten that first night you came to the driving range. I'd never seen an eight-year-old hit the ball like you did. I think you've got a future in golf if you really work at it."

Well, I took the job. Hardy paid me a dollar an hour and I worked six days a week, with Monday off. The range was a couple of miles from my house but transportation was no problem. Hardy drove by and picked me up every day and dropped me off in the evening.

Hardy always believed in working hard and doing things right. At the end of World War II he was in charge of a

Japanese prisoner camp on Corregidor and I'll bet it was a first-class operation. When he came back to Dallas he leased some land from the Caruth family and started putting in his driving range in a big field on Lovers Lane, just off Greenville Avenue. Hardy cleared the land, put up lights for night play, set out some yardage signs, stocked a little white frame building with balls and clubs, nailed up his sign and opened for business. By the time I went to work at the range it was a real popular place. People knew they could go there, hit a bucket of balls and have a good time for a fair price.

I liked working for Hardy, but I still was a kid and I would get restless. After a while I saved a little money and bought my first car, a beat-up 1949 Ford, and I liked to show off in it. North Central, the new expressway that ran parallel with old Coit Road in front of the Glen Lakes clubhouse, was a great temptation. I took the mufflers off my Ford because I wanted to make a racket going through the underpasses. A policeman stopped me one night and gave me a ticket for disturbing the peace. I tried to talk myself out of it, telling him my mufflers fell off, but he didn't buy that. It cost me $5, the only traffic ticket I've ever had.

I dressed like the typical teenage boy of the mid-1950s: blue jeans, black leather motorcycle jacket, motorcycle boots, shirts with big, wide collars you could turn up under your ducktails. This was about the time Elvis Presley came along. Kids danced to the Bop but I never went to any dances. To this day I can't even do the two-step. My idea of a good date was going to Deuback's Skating Rink or back to the range to hit more balls.

I had one romance. Her name was Ann and she was a gorgeous young thing. Blonde. Body like a Ferrari and great wheels. We started dating a lot but we kept it a secret from her parents, since I was Mexican and she was Anglo. When they found out about it they almost went mad, but that didn't stop us.

But working weekends bugged me. Everybody else was off

having fun and I was always at the range. Finally, I got fed up. My old friend Johnny Valle and his four brothers wanted me to join their baseball team, so I skipped work one Sunday and played. When I went back to work on Tuesday Hardy was hot.

"Where the hell were you Sunday?" he asked me.

"Playing baseball," I said. He looked at me real hard. "Are you going to play golf or are you going to play baseball?" he said. "You have to make up your mind."

Then I got mad. "I'm going to play baseball," I said. That was it. I quit.

It was 1956, I was sixteen, and the next few months were very upsetting to me. That fall I found work at River Hills Country Club in Irving, a little town about fifteen miles from where I lived, but nothing was going right. My car broke down and I was having a hard time getting there. And one day when I did, I pulled something I've been ashamed of ever since.

Another kid and I saw a car in the parking lot with real pretty hub caps, so I had my friend take them off and put them in the back seat of my car. I was really stupid. All I was thinking about was how great they would look on my car.

That night a policeman stopped us on the way home, found the hub caps and made me tell him where I got them. Then he did something really nice, something no policeman probably would do today. He called the club, learned the name of the owner and his address, then made me return the hub caps to the man at his home. He let me go free, figuring that I would learn an important lesson. To this day, that has been the extent of my larceny.

I was the luckiest man in the world. I not only wasn't arrested but also wasn't fired. I don't know why. I should have been fired and barred from the club.

So there I was, confused, unsettled and almost seventeen. I began hoping I could enlist in the Marines, but I was afraid they wouldn't take me because I had only a seventh grade education. But on my birthday, December 1, 1956, I went to the Marine Corps recruiting office, took the test and passed it. I was inducted on December 19 and left for boot training in California.

It may seem strange, leaving home so close to Christmas, but that will give you an idea how poor we were. Christmas was not really important to us then. In our house we didn't have presents or a tree or decorations, so it really didn't make that much difference. December 25 was just another day and I figured I may as well spend it with the Marines.

I hadn't been a Marine twenty-four hours before my mouth had me in trouble.

I flew for the first time going to boot camp. The plane stopped in El Paso to refuel, then went on to San Diego. This probably was the most frightening event of my life but I sure didn't want to show it. I got real loud, wisecracking and laughing a lot on the trip, and by the time we landed and loaded into the truck taking us to the receiving barracks I was talking nonstop. There was a black corporal in charge and I got his attention real quick.

It was eleven o'clock at night, but no one was going to bed yet. First, there was a bucket issue—soap, toothbrush, toothpaste, shampoo—and then a shower. Then we packed our old clothes and put on dungarees to wear until the next morning. Everyone was tired, but this corporal said he wanted three volunteers to clean his office. I happened to be one of them.

Before we started work, though, he lined us up and told us how to stand at attention: Thumb down the seam-line of your trousers, palms in, eyes looking straight ahead. My elbow itched so I scratched it. Next thing I knew I was on the floor. That corporal hit me in the stomach with a right hook, then glared down at me.

"When I tell you to stand at attention," he said, "don't breathe."

I didn't learn too fast. The next day they taught us to march and I was laughing and giggling. I got hit in the stomach and slapped in the head so many times I lost count. I was always wild and loud. I had heard that the Indians never killed a crazy man. It was against their religion. I figured that might be true with the Marines, too.

Late one afternoon it was getting cold as the sun went down, so I built a fire in the door of a Quonset hut. Some of us started drinking whiskey and dancing around the fire. I got office hours for that: no liberty for a week and I had to initial my name on the duty roster every hour before bedtime. We had to get out of bed at five every morning and run a mile. Many mornings I slept late, answered roll call in my underwear and wearing no shoes. So I had to run the whole mile that way. *Ooh! Aah! Ooh!* Everyone laughed at me.

Still, I learned a lot during those four months of boot camp. They were probably the happiest moments of my young life because I finally was spending all my time with people my own age. There were eighty or eighty-five guys in our platoon and we worked together, ate together, played games together.

This also was where I was introduced to the Catholic religion. My mother went to church, but I never had gone with her. In the Marines I went to classes and learned something about the religion. I still don't know it very well now, but I know it much better than I did.

And I also learned how a lot of young Marines wind up with tattoos. When I finished boot camp and went home on leave I had two on my right arm. On the forearm was "Ann" for my girl friend. We were exchanging letters and pictures and I thought I was in love. On my biceps was the Devildog, the Marine Corps symbol. I can't tell you where I got that one. I was on liberty and drunk, and there were more tattoo parlors than bars in San Diego. But I know exactly how that first one happened.

Some guy in the barracks could do tattoos, so one night I stuck out my arm and told him to write Ann on it. He took a ball-point pen, wrote her name and then traced it by pushing an ink-soaked thread under my skin with a needle. Hey, I was real proud of the tattoo until I got back to Dallas on leave and Ann wouldn't see me. She had fallen for another guy.

I looked at it and realized it was a mistake, but I've never taken it off. When I made it big on the golf tour the tattoo became a source of mystery to the public because for years I wore a Band-Aid over it when I played.

Somebody would ease up to me, reach for the Band-Aid, and say, "Let me look under there." I'd cover it with my hand and say, "No, you can't see that." People always thought I had a dirty picture or a bad word on my arm until I finally admitted it was a girl's name. Then I told them my wife wouldn't allow me on the tour unless I covered it. A few years later, I got tired of wearing the Band-Aid. Then people asked, "Why did you take it off?" "Well," I said, "I've made so damn much money that now my wife doesn't care if both arms are tattooed."

My twenty-day leave after boot camp was pretty disappointing. I rode a bus four days from San Diego to Dallas, only to find my girl friend had ditched me, and there was so much rain I couldn't get my old Ford out of the mud in the pasture around our house. When I got back to San Diego, I boarded a troop ship bound for duty in Japan. We were on that ship twenty-two days and I've never been so sick in my life. It took so long to reach Japan I thought they were using oars to get us there.

Once we reached Yokohama, though, I was excited again. I had requested infantry duty overseas, thinking it would be the only way I would ever see the world. Never did I dream that someday I'd see it with a set of golf clubs.

I was assigned to Delta Company, 9th Battalion, 3rd Marine Division at Middle Camp Fuji as a machine gunner. I became an expert with the light .30-caliber machine gun. I could take it apart and put it together blindfolded, just like I could the .45 pistol, M-1 rifle and submachine gun. You have to know how to do that in case you're in combat in the dark and your weapon malfunctions or breaks. You can replace the part by feel.

There was no conflict and no combat while I was a Marine. We just trained. I ran up and down those hills around Fuji with that machine gun all day, but sometimes we had some fun at night.

All the buildings outside the base were houses of ill repute and you could go to bed with a girl for two dollars. If you had an overnight pass, you could stay all night with her for $5. A few years ago I was in Japan to play in a tournament at Gotimba and my wife and I rode past that old base. But all those buildings outside had changed. There was a bank, a grocery store, a hotel and lots of shops up and down the road. I laughed and told my wife, "Baby, when that camp was full of Marines there were some fast beds around here." That's just how it was then. You were young, crazy and had never been away from home.

We shipped out to Okinawa in late 1957. We ran more hills and kept training. We practiced amphibious and helicopter landings in the Philippines for a while and finally my eighteen-month Far East tour was finished. I went home for a thirty-day leave, then went back to California for reassignment at Camp Pendleton. I served in an honor guard a while but it was too much spit and polish for me. I wanted something different, so I decided to extend my three-year enlistment a year and request more duty on Okinawa. I did, and then, through some clerical error, I got the luckiest break of my life.

Everyone who was shipped to Okinawa in my group was a corporal, an E-3, but I had orders assigning me to mess duty while all the others went to reconnaissance. This didn't make sense, because in the Marines no one with the rank of corporal or above pulls mess duty. Guys were making fun of me, like I was dumb or being punished, so I went to see the commanding officer, a captain.

"I'm on mess duty and I have no business there," I said. He agreed.

"Do you play any sports?" he asked me. "Yes, sir, I play golf," I said. "Fine," he said. "We'll put you in Special Services."

So for my last eighteen months in the Marines I played a lot of golf. I had a good job, issuing athletic equipment and driving the football team to games in a big six-wheel truck, but the main thing I did was play golf with the officers every afternoon. At noon they would send a driver in a sedan to pick me up and take me to the golf course. I still had to make all formal inspections and had some duties, like NCO-of-the-Day once a month, but overall the job was easy. I stayed in good condition, though. I ran five miles a day and didn't chase around on liberty—well, not very much.

I qualified for the golf team and had quite a bit of success. We traveled a lot to Japan and the Philippines, hopping rides in C-130s and Flying Boxcars, and we won all the interservice tournaments. I won the Okinawa club championship and the Okinawa Chamber of Commerce championship and I got to thinking I was pretty good. Then I met Orville Moody, the best player in the Far East.

He was a sergeant in the Army, the golf director at Camp Zoma in Japan, when we blew in there for a tournament. He was sitting in the lounge, a stocky guy with wavy brown hair, dark eyes and high cheekbones. Orville is from Oklahoma and I think he has a little Indian blood. Well, I walked up to him and said, "I've heard a lot about you. Do you want to play?"

He looked at me a minute. "Who are you?" he asked.

"Corporal Lee Trevino," I told him. "I came to play in the tournament."

"I'm not much of a talker," Orville said. "I let my clubs do the talking."

"Well, let's go out and play for five dollars," I said. But he told me, "You can't beat me. I don't want to take your money."

Hey, that got to me. "What the hell are you talking about?" I said.

He smiled. "Tell you what I'll do. Just to make it more interesting, I'll play you and your partner's best ball." I laughed. "You gotta be joking," I said.

He wasn't. Ed Percival was our number one player, I was number two and Orville did beat our best ball. And he won the tournament by 18 strokes over a Navy captain. I was third, 19 behind Orville.

I told him that day in 1959 he should get out of the Army and go on the tour. But he stayed in the Army and didn't come on the tour until 1967, when he was thirty-four. He wasted eight of his best years. He was ready to play when I first met him. He was seasoned. He had guts. He had nerve. And he could do one thing he can't do now. He could really putt. To this day Orville Moody could win two or three tournaments a year if he could putt.

Maybe he lost his confidence. A lot of times a guy will see somebody else making all the putts and he can't stand it. He wonders why he can't make them and it works in reverse on him. I've had the attitude in putting that only two things can happen. Either the ball goes in or it misses. There's no sense trying to second-guess every little move and that's the way I've always played the game.

Orville had a background similar to mine. I just can't understand why he never had the same attitude. After that one big year in 1969, when he won the U.S. Open and the World Series of Golf and had a lot of high finishes, he dropped back and started struggling. Now he's the pro at a little country club at Sulphur Springs, in East Texas. For some reason, he was trying too hard to beat people all those years out there.

Still, looking back on that day we met, just think how incredible the odds would have been on two guys in that lounge winning back-to-back U.S. Open championships. Damn, I'd have loved to bet $5 on that!

I was discharged at Treasure Island, outside San Francisco, on November 10, 1960, the 185th birthday of the Marine Corps. I was a buck sergeant, what they call lance corporal now, and the service had been good experience for me even if my top pay was only $91 a month. I had been sending $50 a month to my mother and managed to save $900 for myself. I went to San Francisco and caught a bus to Dallas, a milk run that went down through Los Angeles and then across the desert through El Paso. I got home five days later feeling like I had become one of the best the Marines had. My lack of education seemed to make me try a little bit harder than anyone else. I've always been that way.

And I did learn discipline and a strong feeling about defending my country. That's why it made me so damn mad when the Iranians stormed our embassy in 1979 and held all those Americans hostage for so long. Marines guard all U.S. embassies around the world and every Marine learns one thing that applies wherever you are stationed. You protect all government property.

If I had been a guard at the U.S. embassy in Iran, I would be dead today because I would have shot everybody coming through that gate. I can't understand why they let those students break in there and then why our government didn't act immediately to get them out. I guarantee you if Harry Truman had been in the White House we wouldn't have had any problem. Truman would have gone into Iran the next day.

I've been invited to the White House by four Presidents—Richard Nixon, Gerald Ford, Jimmy Carter and Ronald Reagan—but I wish I could have met Harry Truman. I think I would have gotten along great with that man. Everyone in the world respected our country when he was President. He never backed off from anything, and I like that. No way would he ever have been penalized for slow play. He'd just step up and knock the hell out of the ball.

4.
The Great Circle

The five years after my discharge from the Marines saw a lot of changes in my life. I developed a golf game good enough for the tour while working for Hardy Greenwood and playing at Tenison Park. I had two marriages, one divorce and two kids. But I wound up the same way I started. Broke.

When I came home I didn't need very long to spend the $900 I had saved. I wanted to catch up on my drinking and I made a helluva race of it until I ran out of money. Then I needed a job, so Louis Shawver hired me to help him build the second nine holes on the new golf course at the Columbian Club.

I had learned how to build a course when I was fifteen and working for Hardy. He leased the property next to his driving range, on the corner of Lovers Lane and Greenville Avenue, and we built a 9-hole pitch 'n' putt. We did it during the winter and it took us three months—Hardy, his handy man Norman Scott and I. We did all the top dressing, mixed the sand and loam and peat moss to put on the greens, and put in the irrigation system—digging ditches, laying pipes and welding them together. When we finished it was the prettiest little par-3 course you'd ever see.

We put in long hours but we worked on it just five days a week. Hardy and I spent Saturday and Sunday at the driving range. Every Monday morning we would get to the par-3 bright and early ready to work, and Norman Scott wouldn't show up. So I'd jump in Hardy's pickup and go get him. Norman liked to live fast when he wasn't working and usually had a big weekend. I had been out with him some so I knew how he was. He was a helluva guy and a great friend. Hardy took care of me during the day and Norman Scott took care of me during the night.

Now it was December 1960 and I was out building another course. I hadn't asked Hardy for a job. There was no problem with the argument we'd had when I quit before I joined the Marines, but Hardy was busy selling Christmas trees, something he started while I was gone.

I felt good working for Louis, though, because I had been on his crew when he was greens superintendent at Glen Lakes and his son, Jack, was one of my oldest friends. The Columbian Club paid me $250 a month for general labor on the course, mowing greens, raking bunkers and anything else that was needed. I was going full blast: working all day, then drinking beer and raising hell at night. I didn't eat much and by June of 1961 my weight had dropped to about one hundred and forty pounds—thirty less than I weighed in the Marines.

Then Norman Scott dropped by, just like he did when I was fourteen. When he showed up, I knew Hardy wanted to talk to me.

Hardy was curious about my intentions.

"I'm just having fun," I told him.

"Well, are you going to be a laborer the rest of your life or do you want to play golf?" he asked me. "Why don't you come back to work for me and start practicing? You have the ability to be a professional golfer and a good one. You can work nights and have your days free to play golf."

I wasn't wild about working nights because I liked chasing around; but I thought about what Hardy said and decided I should take the job, even though Louis Shawver had the Columbian Club offer me a $100-a-month raise to stay there. With Hardy, I cleared $71 a week after taxes, so there wasn't much difference in the money. The difference was in how I would spend my time. Probably the best decision I ever made was to go back to work for Hardy.

That's when I turned pro, joined the North Texas chapter of the PGA and started playing in a lot of pro-ams during my free time. I won quite a few of them, playing courses like Lakewood, DAC and Glen Lakes in Dallas, and Glen Gardens and Diamond Oaks in Fort Worth. I loved playing so much that once when they didn't have enough pros at Diamond Oaks I played with one group in the morning, another in the afternoon and shot 66–66. That was quite a day. Byron Nelson also played in that pro-am and I met him for the first time.

Everything was fine with Hardy and me. I worked at the driving range and the par-3 course on alternate nights and played a lot of golf. Hardy helped me get a car—a 1958 Oldsmobile. He bought it and I paid him for it out of my weekly checks. Hardy actually was grooming me to go on the tour, preparing me for the day I could qualify for a player's card. But on the side he introduced me to the Christmas tree business.

He had gotten into it accidentally. Two truckers from Montana hauled some trees into town and parked their semis almost on the fairway of the pitch 'n' putt course one rainy December night when they checked into a motel across the street. Next morning their trucks were stuck and they were frantic. Hardy was mad at first but then, having a good business mind, he said, "Why don't you unload your trees on my lot? I'll get a permit to sell them and we'll split the money fifty-fifty."

That worked out pretty good, so the next winter Hardy made a deal with a nursery in Montana. He let the nursery people park their trucks on his property and use his clubhouse for an office. He got first choice of the trees on consignment. Now you can't beat that with an ugly stick, getting them on consignment. After that, Hardy was in the Christmas tree business in a big way.

When I came back we built two sheds, put flocking machines in them and I started spraying trees with rubber-based paint, which looked like snow on the limbs when it dried. Once I worked twenty-seven straight hours and flocked five hundred trees. People paid top dollar for them, but they got their money's worth because it was very difficult work. One of the biggest trees I ever flocked was a thirty-two-foot balsam that went in the lobby of the Medical Arts Building downtown. It was a gorgeous tree, but we had a very tough time getting it in there.

The Christmas tree season was something I looked forward to, since no one was playing much golf at that time of year and this kept us busy. God, it got cold out there selling those trees, but we drank a lot of beer and whiskey and stayed at it. I always worked late, just like I did at the driving range and par-3. I even stayed until midnight on Christmas Eve, because some people liked to buy a tree when their kids were asleep, take it home and decorate it to surprise them the next morning.

That was Hardy, Norman and me—Santa's helpers.

My social life was pretty limited once I started working nights but that didn't keep me from meeting Linda, the girl who became the first Mrs. Trevino.

Her kid brother hung around the driving range, and since he was about thirteen, I believe he wanted to get some attention from the older guys. "Why don't you take my sister out?" he asked me and once I saw her—a brunette about five three with a cute smile—I said, "Well, why don't I?" It was the summer of 1961. I was twenty-one and she was seventeen, a senior at North Dallas High School. Her father was dead, and when I met her mother and sister they didn't seem to object to me. But her uncle sure as hell did. He wanted to break us up because I was Mexican and she was Anglo.

We kept dating, though, usually just going to a bowling alley or taking a six-pack of beer to a drive-in movie. By November we decided we wanted to get married, but she was underage and didn't have her parents' consent. We pulled a fast one, putting water on her birth certificate so the numbers blurred, making the year of her birth, 1944, look like 1942. Then we drove ninety miles up to Durant, Oklahoma, found a justice of the peace and got married. Jack Shawver and his wife, Ann, went with us.

We kept it secret until the Christmas holidays, and then told her mother. All hell broke loose. My Uncle Joe had a small house in Garland, so I rented that, fixed it up a little with a new carpet and such, and transferred my wife to Garland High School to finish her senior year. By the time she graduated she was pregnant. And on November 21, 1962, our son Richard Lee was born.

I wasn't around too much, however. By then I was swept up in playing golf every day at Tenison Park.

Ah, Tenison Park. It may be the most famous municipal course in the world and I've had something to do with that. But a lot of people are confused about how long I played there. After I won the U.S. Open in 1968 a story went around that I learned to play golf at Tenison as a little boy. The truth is I never set foot there until the summer of 1961 when I was twenty-one. But once I did, I knew it was my kind of place.

I had played a lot of golf at Bob-O-Links, another East Dallas course operated by Harry McCommas and his son, Hal, and I liked it there. But Tenison was special. It was only a ten-minute drive from Hardy's and had 36 holes that really tested my game. A lot of different people played there and they mixed well together. It was kind of like a big family and I felt very comfortable. It was always exciting. Tenison had a tremendous influence on my play, and my life. It always will be one of my favorite courses.

It's a rolling layout, with thousands of pecan trees and an old cream-colored clubhouse sitting on a hill between Samuell Boulevard and East Grand Avenue. Erwin Hardwicke was the pro for years and he was the perfect host. Your background didn't matter. If you could pay the greens fee, you went out and played and had fun.

Lee Elder also played there as a young man when he was as poor as I was. A lot of wealthy people played there, some for fun, some for big money. Tenison was the only golf course I've ever seen where the parking lot was filled with Cadillacs, jalopies, pickups and beverage trucks. A friend who worked for a bottling company went by Tenison to play every morning. Then he'd work like hell in the afternoon to deliver those soft drinks.

Tenison was the hardest "easy" course I ever played. It had only one bunker—to the left of the 18th hole on the East course—but it had such length and such character that it didn't need any. There were so many trees, which made it a very difficult golf course. When the U.S. Public Links championship was played at Tenison, they let the rough grow and the winning score was something like 13 over par. It has big greens, but it's just so difficult. It was the perfect place to sharpen my game.

Tenison is also where I met Arnold Salinas, the greatest friend I've ever had. People in the Pan American Golf Association told me Arnold was the best Mexican-American player in Dallas while I was in the Marines and then they told him how good I was. They kept trying to get us together but I always went to Tenison at six in the morning and he came later. Then there was a pro-am one Monday and damned if we didn't draw each other. We won, shooting 13 under, and I was low pro. I believe I beat Arnold by a stroke. I asked him if he could play the next morning. He said, "Look, you'll have to come by and pick me up if you want me on any golf course at six in the morning."

That was fine with me. I just wanted to play as much golf as possible. So the next morning I walked right into the Salinases' house and into Arnold's bedroom, woke him up and we went to Tenison. I think I woke up the whole family but no one got mad at me. I guess they just figured I was crazy.

They're a great family—five sons, two daughters and a wonderful father and mother. Andrew Salinas took great pride in his sons' golfing ability, but the first time I met him I told him none of them could beat me. So the next day he brought Arnold and Albert and I beat their best ball. Mr. Salinas looked at me and said, "You *can* play." Since then, he and Mama Angie Salinas have been like father and mother to me. I worship them and take them with me on trips all over the world. I not only built my game at Tenison but found a family.

Some wild stories have me winning thousands of dollars gambling on the golf course at Tenison, but it never happened. Sure there were some very big games, but I didn't have the money to get in them. The biggest bet I ever made in those days was $5, but that's big enough if you don't have a penny in your pocket.

The big-money players were a fascinating bunch of guys. The most famous was Titanic Thompson, but there were plenty more who loved action—Arthur Corbin, Jack Keller, Joe Campisi and some I just knew by names like Ace and Fat Mickey. And there was Dick Martin, probably the best player I ever saw until Jack Nicklaus.

Dick would have been great on the tour but he was just a little early. He came from the Ben Hogan era, and I guess the tour, which didn't have big purses then, didn't appeal to him when he could make so much money at Tenison. He was a little guy, only five five or so, but he had more shots and was as accurate as anyone I've seen. And he wasn't scared of anyone.

He also was a great creator of games. People congregated around him, anxious to play with him because he could think of so many ways to bet. Sometimes Dick took a couple of dozen guys out to play in the snow. They painted their golf balls with Mercurochrome. Sometimes they played with baseball bats.

Then there was the Tunnel Game, where you each put up $25, took one club and went out to the farthest point of the course. You tried to hit your ball back to the clubhouse across the front nine on the East course, but you had to go through a concrete tunnel under the railroad track between the Number 2 tee and Number 1 green. If you hit over it, you had to come back and knock your ball through that tunnel, which was a narrow, forty-foot walkway. If a guy didn't put his ball in the right position, he might take 12 or 13 getting through it. You could hear some fantastic cussing around that tunnel.

They played one called Honest John, where you paid every other player $10 for each stroke you took. If you had a bad day, you could lose a tremendous amount of money. Another was called Trees: you paid every other player $10 for each tree you hit. At Tenison, with all those pecan trees, that could get pretty damn expensive. And if your ball bounced off one tree and hit another, you paid each guy $20.

Then there were the regular big-money games, where they finally went out and played after sitting in the clubhouse half the day drinking coffee and trying to outhustle each other. They usually just played nine holes because they spent so much time arguing and bullshitting, trying to get strokes and win the match before they ever teed off.

They played what we called The Cutback on the East course: 1, 2, 3, 4, 5 and then over to 15, 16, 17 and 18. The course could be full and three or four players might be on the 14th hole when you'd see a gang coming down Number 5— maybe a half dozen of the biggest gamblers in Dallas with fifteen or twenty people following them in carts. Next thing you knew, they'd jump over in front of you on 15. No one would dare say anything to them. No telling how much artillery they had under their jackets and in their socks and golf bags.

You couldn't blame them for not getting too far out. There had been hold-ups in the back corner of the course when robbers took thousands of dollars.

There's a great story about one of those robberies. When the gamblers got back on the 8th hole two guys came out of the trees with shotguns. Before one guy handed over his money, he counted out $1,000 and handed it to another victim. "Here," he said. "We're even."

I got into only one big game with those guys before I went on the tour. That was in 1965 when the Fat Man, Martin Stanovich, came to town. He dropped by Hardy's to offer me a deal. I knew him by reputation, a golf gambler from Chicago who looked for big games.

"I want to go to Tenison and play Dick Martin and some of those other guys," he told me, "and I want you for a partner. I'll put up all the money. All I want you to do is help me with club selection and read the greens for me. I know that you're not a big gambler and you don't play with them, so I know you won't put me in the middle."

I told him he didn't have to put up any money for me, that I'd play with him just for pleasure. Well, we played the West course with Dick, Erwin Hardwicke, Hal McCommas and two or three others, and he beat them all with my help. He was a fine player, even if he didn't look like one.

The Fat Man was about five ten and two hundred and forty pounds, and he wore a big, old, ugly Panama hat pulled down on the right side of his head like Al Capone. He had the left side up so he could see how to swing, but he looked terrible hitting the ball. He used Croyden clubs with grips twice as long as normal and he'd choke way down on them. He had a God-awful swing. He held the club way out in front of him and when he hit the ball he'd fall back on his right foot. But it was a come-on. If you're a golf hustler, you've got to have some gimmicks. You can't look good. Well, he sure didn't look good but he could play. He lives in Florida now and I see him there all the time. We still enjoy talking about his trip to Tenison.

As for me, I never hustled a soul at Tenison. A hustler is a golfer who lies about his handicap. Hell, I didn't have a handicap. I always said I was a scratch player. Of course, I shot 66, 67 or 68, but I didn't call that hustling, just good playing. Besides, who could I find to hustle at six in the morning?

When Ricky was a few months old we moved into an apartment on Shadyside Lane, just across East Grand from Tenison, so I could get to the course sooner. I wore Bermuda shorts or cut-off jeans, old T-shirts and sometimes I went barefoot. If the mosquitoes were biting, I'd go into the creek and pack mud on my legs and arms to keep them off, something I learned in the Marines. I looked like hell. My golf bag was a little $2.95 canvas job with a hole in the bottom, so I carried it on my shoulder like a rifle or across my back. If I had carried it the usual way all of my clubs would have fallen out the bottom.

I would walk across East Grand to the 14th tee on the West course and start playing from there. I could play 18 holes by ten and have time for more before I went home to shower, eat lunch, and get to work at Hardy's by two. Usually I played with Arnold Salinas, Howard Buchanan and Bobby Moreland, and as I said, we never played for much because we didn't have much—a dollar a side, a twenty-five-cent bet here or there and low score taking a dollar from everyone else. If they didn't show up by six-thirty, I'd tee off alone.

I didn't have to have a game with someone else. I'd hit two

balls, pretending one was Ben Hogan's. Ben Hogan never won a match. His ball always was the one that missed the green or a short putt.

In reality, the toughest player at Tenison was Dick Martin. I did beat him quite badly once, shooting 62 on the East course. He was a very smart player and when he saw I was having an excellent day he quit betting on 14. I won $100, the best day I ever had at Tenison before I went on the tour.

Later, when I had plenty of money, I'd come back and play three of them—Dick, Erwin and maybe one of the assistant pros. I was betting $75 and they were betting $25 apiece with automatic one-down presses—if you lost a hole you had to start a new bet. It's difficult to beat three good players like that and I only won one game. I lost as much as $1,000 on 18 holes but, what the hell, I had the money. It was fun doing it, with all those people following us. And we were lucky. We never got held up.

The action was good at Hardy's, too. I came up with a lot of gimmick bets there, but the one that has become most famous was playing with a Dr Pepper bottle.

I started that accidentally. I had a family-size bottle, a 32-ounce size with very thick glass, and I was fooling around with it at the driving range, throwing balls up and hitting them. I did pretty well so I started practicing with it. I broke one and nicked my hand, so I came up with a solution. I wore a glove on my right hand and wrapped adhesive tape around the neck of the bottle so I wouldn't cut my hand if it broke. I got better and better with it, so I went to the pitch 'n' putt and played with it. I knocked the ball on the green, then putted croquet style, crouching and swinging the bottle between my legs. I was good, but I practiced with it almost a year before I got into a match. Then I played with that bottle for three years and never lost to someone playing with a club.

My first match was with a fat little insurance salesman who loved that par-3 course and would not play unless I played with him. He wore clothes from the Roaring Twenties, always had his hat sideways like the Fat Man and carried a big wad of money. He worked in the poor black and Mexican communities, collecting weekly premiums, and he kept about 300 dollar bills rolled up with a $100 bill around them. He couldn't stand it if he didn't come by two or three times a week to play me on the pitch 'n' putt and drop $10 or $15 each time. He was a solid loser, this man.

He'd say, "There aren't too many people who can play like me on this par-3, are there?" "No," I'd say, figuring to butter him up and bring him back. Maybe I hustled the guy, but I never stuck a gun to his head. He wanted to gamble. He went for anything. He was a natural for the Dr Pepper bottle.

When I was working I would only play the first and ninth holes, the two closest to the clubhouse, so if somebody drove up I could run back and wait on them. The insurance salesman came by one afternoon and said, "Let's play a couple of holes." "No," I said. "Hell, you can't beat me."

"But you know I'm good," he said. "Yeah, but you can't beat me with my club." I hesitated, then I said, "Hey, I've got a new deal for you. You might have a chance to win. I'm going to play you with this bottle and you give me the ties."

"What do you mean, ties?" he asked. "If I tie you on the hole, I win it," I said. He grinned. "You've got it."

Well, he parred the two holes but so did I, so I won. After that I asked for half a stroke a hole when I played with the Dr Pepper bottle. I thought I deserved some edge.

The little guy never could understand how I always won. "I think I can do that," he said. "Let me try." He'd throw the ball up and whiff it every time. I had the eye-hand coordination to hit it, but he didn't.

I also won money betting people I could hit the 100-yard sign on the range. I was so good with my 9-iron that sometimes I'd say, "The zero or the one?" But the best one I had with that 9-iron was shooting at a little sprinkler 110 yards away. I'd bet people I could hit that sprinkler one out of ten times and I did.

While I was succeeding at golf, I was failing at marriage. Linda called me a golf bum and we had some big arguments about my being gone so much.

"Either it's going to be golf or it's going to be Ricky and me," she said. "We don't know you. You never take us anyplace. Why don't you get an eight to five job like everyone else?"

In the fall of 1963 she left me. She took Ricky and moved in with her sister, who was separated from her husband. She took a job downtown and filed for divorce. I was terribly depressed. When that deputy sheriff served me the papers, I felt like I was being arrested for murder.

I realize now that we got married out of puppy love, a love of passion. I wasn't ready for it and I just did what I wanted. I was having my cake and eating it, too. The golf-marriage ratio was 90–10. But once they were gone, it hurt. On Monday, my day off, I'd pick up Ricky at the nursery and take him to Tenison, where I'd putt one-handed while he rode on my hip. In November, when Ricky was one year old, the divorce was final. Judge Sarah T. Hughes of Domestic Relations Court, the lady who swore in Lyndon Johnson as President after John Kennedy was assassinated, instructed me to pay $30 a week for child support. An attorney named Jerry Beezel handled my case. His fee was two dozen golf balls. He knew I didn't have any money and he really didn't have to do much. We didn't have anything to split up.

I was heartbroken for a while. I moved back to that old house with my grandfather; he noticed I was upset and had lost a lot of weight. "Son," he told me, "the only way to forget a woman is with another one." He was right.

In February Ray Curley, a buddy who was assistant pro at Riverlake Country Club, asked me if I wanted a blind date with a girl named Claudia Fenley, a neighbor of the girl he was dating. She was a cute, slender blonde and she was seventeen. She lived with her mother, had dropped out of high school her senior year and was selling tickets at the Capri Theater downtown. We went to the Cotton Bowling Palace, but she hated bowling so I took her home early. I figured that was it.

But in April she called the driving range and I answered the phone. "This is Claudia," she said. "Who?" I asked. "Claudia," she said. Well, we talked a few minutes and that night she came by the range with Ray Curley and his girl friend. They helped me pick up balls and waited while I closed the range, then we went out and had a couple of beers.

We started going out a lot, double-dating with Arnold Salinas after I finished work at Hardy's. We went to clubs all over town following a popular local group called the Panthers. I really liked their music. One night I got to feeling so good I jumped up on the stage and started dancing with them. Arnold and I laughed about how those girls must have thought we were rich. They didn't know we were spending every nickel we'd won at the course that day. Sometimes we stayed out all night, so Arnold and I headed straight to Tenison at dawn. We were broke and hung over, but pretty soon we were ready to play again.

During the summer Clyde and I decided to get married. I was twenty-four and she was still seventeen, but her mother, Lou, had no objection and she was her legal guardian. Her father, Claude Fenley, had remarried some years earlier and had some young children by a wife about my age.

Hardy was totally against our marriage, just as he was against my first one. He believed I wasn't mature enough to handle the responsibility of that first marriage and now, less than a year after the divorce, I had found another young wife. But I didn't talk to him about it. I just went ahead.

August 17, 1964, was to be our wedding day. I picked that date because it was a Monday, my day off. I went to Zale's Jewelers on East Grand and bought Clyde a wedding band

and a tiny little diamond ring for $186 on credit. I mean that diamond was *tiny*! But when I gave it to her she thought it was the most gorgeous thing she had ever seen.

Then I told her we'd have to postpone the wedding a week. I got an invitation to play in a pro-pro event in Fort Worth on August 17 at Glen Gardens, the old club where Ben Hogan and Byron Nelson once caddied. Clyde never had seen me play a complete round of golf, so she went with me. I remember how she looked that day, wearing a pink sun dress with her hair done up nice.

I played probably the most flawless round of my life, an 11-under-par 61 for a course record that still stands. The day was to be a special send-off for two young pros—Dewitt Weaver, Jr., and Dudley Wysong—who were starting on the tour, but I won top money, $300. That was almost like getting a month's salary!

Weaver and Wysong shot 68 or 69, and when it was announced that I had won with a 61, they took some razzing from the other pros: "Hey, maybe we're sending the wrong guys on the tour!"

Driving home that night, we got a six-pack for the road. I was feeling great and then Clyde asked me, "Was that good today?" I shot a 61 and she wanted to know if it was good!

"Yeah," I told her, "that's the lowest round I've ever played." She wasn't impressed.

"How many birdies did you have?" she asked.

"I had an eagle and nine birdies," I said.

"What's good?" she asked.

"Eagles are good, but they're very difficult to get," I said. "But birdies are good, too. The more birdies you can get, the better off you are."

"Well, how many holes are there on the course?" she asked.

"Eighteen," I said.

"Well," she said, "why can't you birdie all eighteen?"

I looked at her. "Do what?" I asked.

"I'm not ever going to be satisfied," she told me, "until you birdie all eighteen in one round."

I didn't say any more. I just opened another beer and kept driving. "Baby," I thought to myself, "you may have to wait a little while for that."

I didn't have a sports coat, tie or anything nice to wear, so with my new wealth I went to Sears and bought myself some wedding clothes. I paid $26 for a coat, $1.50 for a tie and $2.99 for a white shirt. I wore that with a pair of my golf slacks when we got married. I didn't wear my golf shoes, though. I had a pair of regular dress shoes.

I looked in the phone book, found the name of a retired minister in Oak Cliff and called him. I said we wanted to get married the next Monday and he asked at what time. I told him four in the afternoon. I wanted to play golf first.

We drove over to Oak Cliff and finally found this little two-room house where the preacher lived. To this day I don't know if he was Baptist or Methodist. He was a little man of about seventy-five, and since nobody came to our wedding, he called his little wife out as a witness.

There was nothing little about his service, though. He started giving us the whole sermon. I had expected it to be real brief, like my first marriage ceremony, when we stood by a sink in an office with fifty people beating on typewriters. That justice of the peace in Oklahoma said something like, "Do you, Linda, take Lee for your husband? Do you, Lee, take Linda for your wife? You're married. Give me two dollars."

But this little man carried on for fifteen minutes, telling us about the holy bond of matrimony. When he finally married us, I asked him what I owed him. He told me whatever I'd like to give him. I handed him $25, grabbed Clyde's hand and said, "Let's go. I want a drink." Arnold, who was working in a liquor store on Industrial Boulevard near the Sportatorium, the old wrestling arena, had invited us to come by for a celebration.

He took us in the back room, where he had stacked six cases of beer for a table and put four cases around for seats. He opened a bottle of champagne, poured glasses for Clyde, me, the store manager and himself and we drank a toast. Then he called El Fenix Restaurant and told Irene Martinez, the owner, that he was sending us by to have dinner. He also ordered us a bottle of champagne, but Irene wouldn't serve it to Clyde because she was seventeen.

That night we went to the Blackout, a club where the Panthers were playing, and had a great time. There was no time for a honeymoon. The next day I went back to work for Hardy, who still thought our marriage was a bad idea.

Hardy hadn't lost interest in my future, though. He was always encouraging me.

In the summer of 1963 he took me to DAC to see the PGA Championship. It was my first glimpse of a big tournament and the first time I watched Jack Nicklaus, who won it. Hardy sent me to PGA Business School for two weeks, which gave me one year of credit toward the five years of club professional work I needed to earn a Class A card and join the tour under the more difficult rules in effect then. And a few weeks after we got married I played in the Dallas Open at Oak Cliff Country Club on a sponsor's exemption, thanks to Hardy's contacts with tournament officials.

I made the cut after 36 holes, when the field was reduced to 60 low scores and ties, and although I didn't win any money I got to play with Julie Boros in the third round. I was terribly nervous. To this day I don't remember hitting the ball off the first tee. It was Saturday and there was a big gallery. I shot 74, but Boros was impressed with how I made the ball bump and run.

When I played Hardy's par-3 course I never landed the ball on the green. I always bumped it into the bank, let it hop up and then trickle up a few feet from the pin. So every time I missed a green at Oak Cliff I took a pitching wedge and left the ball about a foot from the hole. Boros shook his head and said, "Son, I've never seen anybody do that before. You do it every time?" "Every time," I said. I hoped that soon I would be doing that in a lot of tour events.

By the summer of 1965 I had enough years to qualify for a Class A card and I was excited. Our daughter Lesley was born on June 30 and we were hard pressed for money, but I had some guys who wanted to sponsor me on the tour. I filled out the PGA application for a Class A card and took it to Hardy for his signature. As my employer, he had to verify I had worked four years for him in addition to attending PGA Business School for one year's credit.

Hardy wouldn't sign it. He believed I wasn't ready, that I was too wild and immature to handle the responsibility of traveling all over the country and playing professional golf. I guess he had good reason to think that. He had sent me to a tournament in Lake Charles, Louisiana, and had given me $600 to cover my expenses. He specifically told me, "Keep a record of every nickel you spend." Instead, I stayed drunk for six days.

I love beer and I could sit on a bar stool for hours and drink one after another. But I thought the Louisiana law was like Texas law was then, and told myself, "I'll just sit here until they close the door at midnight." But in Louisiana they serve twenty-three hours a day. It would be four or five in the morning and I'd still be drinking. I played lousy and came home without a cent.

I argued with Hardy when he refused to sign my application, but he just said, "You haven't matured enough to do this." In a moment of anger, I told him, "To hell with it. I quit."

Some of the pros around town like Eldridge Miles, Erwin Hardwicke, Dennis Lavender and Howard Buchanan were behind me one hundred and fifty percent but they couldn't change anything. George Alexander, the president of the North Texas chapter, was sympathetic, but he told me he couldn't approve my application until Hardy signed it.

So I was out of luck and out of work. Clyde found a job as file clerk for an insurance company, but her pay was only $55 a week. I wasn't playing in any pro-ams. I wasn't playing anyplace. I went to Tenison but I never had any money to bet, so I would just hit practice balls . . . maybe two thousand a day.

Then Bill Gray came to me and gave me a great deal. Bill was about my age, a bachelor who loved to gamble. We'd known each other around Tenison a long time and he knew what I could do on the golf course. "I'll sponsor you," he said. "We'll go to Houston and you can play in the Texas State Open. I'll pay expenses and give you sixty percent of what you win."

So we drove down there and I entered. Clyde went, too, and we stayed at the Tidelands Motel, which I thought was the fanciest place I'd ever seen. The Texas State Open had a pretty good field, with players like Homero Blancas, Gay Brewer and Bobby Nichols. Bill Gray got busy betting and I played real well. I beat Frank Wharton in a playoff and won $1,000, which was the most money I'd ever seen in my life. I cashed the check, Bill gave me $600 and we came home happy. He'd killed 'em betting, and because I looked so good in the tournament I was invited to play in the Mexican Open in November.

I was excited but I didn't have any money to throw around. I had been out of work a long time and we owed a lot—rent, furniture, doctors, insurance. Still, some surprising things had happened and all of them were good for me.

Like the phone call from El Paso. Before we went to Mexico City, Clyde and I went to a movie one night while her mother, Lou, stayed with Lesley. When we got home Lou told me, "A man named Don Wilson wants you to call him in El Paso." Don Wilson played the tour a little and did some hustling, which is what he was doing out there. He was calling me from Horizon Hills Country Club and he told me a guy named Martin Lettunich wanted to talk to me.

"I don't know any Martin Lettunich," I told Don Wilson. But what the hell, they were paying for the call so I decided to talk to him. Later I learned that Martin Lettunich is a wealthy man, and a really good guy. He farms thousands of acres of cotton at Fabens, outside of El Paso; he has cattle and he's on the board of two or three banks. And he loves to gamble.

So Martin gets on the phone speaking Spanish. *"Hey, chico, cómo está todo?"*

I said, "Wait a minute. I may be Mexican but I don't speak Spanish that well."

So he said, "Well, let me tell you what I've got here. I asked Don if he knows someone who is an unknown and who can play this game, and he said, 'Yeah, I know one guy, Lee Trevino from Dallas.' Well, we're playing a little golf out here and want to know if you can join us for a couple of days." One of the guys Martin wanted me to play was Fred Hawkins, who was famous for finishing second so much on the tour that he became known as the bridesmaid of the tour.

Clyde was standing beside me. "What is it?" she whispered. I put my hand over the receiver and told her, "This guy wants me to fly to El Paso and play two days against some other guys." "You can't go," Clyde said. "We're leaving for Mexico City in four days." I said, "Honey, this guy is going to send me a round-trip airline ticket, pay my expenses and give me $300." Quick as a snap, Clyde said, "Yeah, tell him you can go."

I took an early-morning flight to El Paso and a friend named Robert Sparks—wearing a cowboy hat and driving a pickup—met me at the airport. I'd played golf with Robert in Dallas, and his mother owned a lot of land north of El Paso. He took me out to Horizon and I looked at the course and played a few holes real quick. The other players would start descending on the club at noon, but Martin Lettunich came early to have coffee with me.

I had a silver golf bag with Lee Trevino written on it.

Probably the greatest thing in the world for a young player is to have a bag with his name on it. I was really proud of that thing. But when Martin saw it he said, "Oh, no, *chico*, we can't have that bag." He went in the storeroom, found a little tattered bag with the bottom falling out and put my clubs in it. "Use this," he said. Then he took me out to hit practice balls before anybody showed up.

In a little while here comes Fred Hawkins. Well, I'm as nervous as a dog eating razor blades. I was wearing a raggedy old shirt and pants with mud all over my shoes, but that was how Martin wanted it. He told me he didn't want me to look good. Then another player, Gene Fisher, showed up.

He introduced me as his tractor driver. "This little kid's been practicing," Martin said, "and I think he can beat y'all." Then Hawkins and Fisher started hitting balls and I was on the putting green when Frank Redman appeared. Frank was a top amateur player and once it was a tossup in El Paso who would go on the tour, him or Hawkins. He also had been a USGA official for years and knew a lot about what was happening throughout golf.

Frank stopped to see Hawkins and asked, "Fred, who are you playing today?" "I don't know," Hawkins told him. "Some little Mexican boy out there on the putting green that Martin brought in here." Redman took one look and said, "Do you have any idea who that kid is? That's Lee Trevino from Dallas. He just won the Texas State Open. Fred, that kid can lay it down." But Hawkins wasn't impressed. "If I've never heard of him," he said, "he can't play."

I ran right over Fred Hawkins those two days, shooting 65 and 67. Martin Lettunich and his friends made a killing betting on me and he was one happy farmer when he gave me the $300 and put me on the plane to Dallas. When I landed, Clyde and Bill Gray were waiting at the airport with the car packed. Bill was living high and had bought a new Oldsmobile Cutlass. We headed straight for Mexico City without going home. It was a great trip. I finished second to Homero Blancas and won $2,100.

When we got back from the Mexican Open, Bill and I were excited about taking off again, this time for Panama, Caracas and Bogotá. We hustled around and got passports, packed up Bill's Olds Cutlass again and headed south, just the two of us. We believed we'd have no problem driving to the Panama Open. Bill had put his fingers on a map, and said, "Lookie here, from Dallas to Mexico City is this far and we drove it in a day and a half. Mexico City to Panama City is about the same distance. We'll be there in three days."

Well, let me tell you something. There ain't roads all the way through. It took us eight days to reach Panama City and every damn thing went wrong. We went through Guatemala, Honduras, El Salvador and Costa Rica and didn't have visas for any of them so we kept doubling back for hours to the consulates where we could get them. We drove through riverbeds and the densest jungle in the world, but that looked a lot better than the hotel in El Salvador we stayed in one night.

We were in a huge room, sort of a dormitory with blackboard partitions separating the beds. It was so hot that I opened a window and then fell asleep. Next thing I knew, there was something on my bed and Bill was slapping at it. I turned on the light and saw it was a huge bat! I jumped up and killed it with my putter and we got out of there. We slept in the car the rest of the way.

One time in the jungle we stopped for a little blockage in the road and a guy just comes out of nowhere. He was wearing khakis and carrying a submachine gun. I said, "Oh, goddamn." If he wanted the car or anything we had, he could have killed us and thrown us out. Well, I tried to be friendly. In my broken Spanish, I said to him, "How you doing?"

He glared at me a minute, then said, *"Dónde van?"*— "Where are you going?" I said we were going to Panama to play golf.

He walked around the car, his hand on that machine gun. Then he said, *"Cigarro?"* I gave him a whole goddamn carton of Parliaments! Then he vanished as quickly as he appeared and we got the hell gone.

When we reached Panama City we were relieved to check into a nice hotel. We stayed at the Panama Hilton, and I won $500 or $600 in the tournament. Bill's car was a shambles so we had to leave it there and fly the rest of the way. I was sitting on my luggage in the hotel lobby, waiting for him so we could check out, when he dragged in after an all-night party. He had spent every nickel we had, but we managed to pay the hotel bill with a credit card and took off. When we wound up in Bogotá I won $600 or so but he blew that, too. He kept bailing us out with that credit card and finally got us two airline tickets to Dallas' Love Field. His mother picked us up at the airport and took me home. When I walked in the door I had been gone a month and I didn't have a cent to show for it. My wife and baby daughter were starving and it was almost Christmas. I didn't know what I was going to do.

Then Martin Lettunich called.

"Remember that boy, Gene Fisher, you met when you were out here?" he asked me. "He thinks he can beat you."

I said, "No, there ain't no way he can beat me." And Martin said, "Well, he thinks about it so strong that he's already made a contract with me to play you on five different courses on five different days. I want you to come out here again."

He paused a moment and said, "Let me ask you something. Are you working there?"

"No," I said.

"Well, why don't you just pack up your wife and your little girl and your belongings and move to El Paso?" he asked me.

"Martin, I don't have a quarter," I told him.

"Don't worry about it, *chico*," he said. "We'll find something for you to do."

5.
El Paso
Connection

El Paso looks as much like Dallas as I look like Jack Nicklaus. It has mountains and desert and the spirit of an old frontier town. In a way it still is, sitting way out in West Texas, smack on the border of Mexico and New Mexico. And it's an awfully long drive from Dallas—650 miles. Hey, that's halfway to Los Angeles.

But I was really excited about making the trip in February 1966 when I loaded Clyde and our baby girl Lesley into my 1958 Oldsmobile and left Dallas. We had sold our furniture for practically nothing, put a few belongings in a rented U-Haul trailer and hitched it to the car. I had $50 in my pocket and that was it. All I had waiting for me was that series of matches Martin Lettunich had arranged with Gene Fisher and the hope of finding a club job that would help me get my Class A card and join the tour. Since I was leaving nothing in Dallas, that was plenty.

El Paso has around 350,000 people, and considering Juárez is just minutes away, the total population of the area may be 800,000 or so. But it's a big, small city, probably one of the friendliest cities I've ever seen. We lived there twelve years and we loved it. Dallas, in its way, is just as friendly but it's so damn big! It's difficult to know a lot of people in Dallas. You may have four or five close friends. In El Paso, you have two hundred.

We learned real quick that we needed to speak Spanish well. It was fun being so close to Mexico. Juárez has some good bars and night clubs, and most important to me, it has a race track. Any time I had a few dollars I loved to bet on the dog races. Years later, after I had won a big tournament, I'd come home and celebrate in the penthouse of Juárez Race Track.

Thousands of people go back and forth every day on the bridges over the Rio Grande, which seems like no river at all most of the time. On a pretty afternoon you can drive over to Juárez and see kids playing baseball, soccer and football in the dry riverbed. It makes you feel good just riding along and watching them.

But when we rolled into El Paso that first day my car was wheezing and we didn't know where we were going to stay. Thanks to Robert Sparks and his mother, we wound up renting a two-bedroom trailer house by the maintenance barn on their ranch. Once we were settled there, I took off to meet Martin Lettunich.

We had an agreement to play five different courses, starting with Coronado Country Club. Gene Fisher, who wanted to play me, was a good golfer and he turned out to be a good friend. We had a tough little time of it that day. My partner was Jesse Whittenton, who had played defensive back for the Green Bay Packers and now was operating Horizon Hills Country Club with his cousin. Gene Fisher's partner was a kid named Steve Summers, a pretty good player for the University of Texas at El Paso. We beat them one up and won $400. Next day we went to Horizon Hills.

It turned into a big blowout for us. There were automatic

presses, forcing the losers to start new bets by the hole, and to this day I don't know how much was won or lost but it must have been a lot. The wind was blowing thirty miles an hour and the dust was flying and tumbleweeds were rolling across the fairways. I shot 65 and Jesse helped me on three holes, so we had 62 best ball. Gene Fisher shot 81 and the kid shot 79, and their best ball was something like 75.

The next day we were supposed to play at the country club in Juárez but they didn't show up, so the deal ended after two matches.

I wasn't nearly as nervous this time as I was when I beat Fred Hawkins. I felt comfortable out there. I really had gotten my game together the past few years in Dallas. Learning to hit a fade like Ben Hogan did had helped a lot. I was a better player, hitting the ball from left to right.

I was hooking the ball real bad when I got out of the Marine Corps, but one day I was invited to play at Shady Oaks, Hogan's club in Fort Worth, with Hardy Greenwood and two other fellows. Hogan was practicing when we arrived, and while I wouldn't dare go near him, I could see how he was hitting the ball. The thing was going out there with a fade, right at the caddie, the caddie never moving.

I'd never hit a fade before, but I went back to the driving range in Dallas and started working on it. The only way I could fade it was to move my body as I swung. I got in the habit of hitting the ball with a big old sway. I hit so many balls that way, you wouldn't believe it, and I grooved a fade, a reliable slider. I had it perfected. And Ben Hogan was the reason I developed the game I have.

But in El Paso I needed a place to practice, play and work toward my Class A card. That turned out to be Horizon Hills, where Jesse and his cousin, Donnie Whittington, really didn't need a club pro but came up with a job for me. Martin Lettunich had talked to Bill Eschenbrenner, the pro at El Paso Country Club, and a lot of other guys in the local PGA chapter and they got busy trying to help me with the technicalities involving my card. Then Martin told Jesse and Donnie, "We gotta find something for him because he's working toward his Class A card."

They hired me as sort of a handy man around the club, but my main job was to open up at five in the morning, because a lot of farmers and railroad workers liked to play early there. Monty Strange, a little guy who had a crippled hand from taking a bullet during a fight, ran the pro shop. He came to work about nine-thirty in the morning and then closed it down at night. My salary was $30 a week, which was good because that was all I wanted to do. I had time to practice and play all day and some days I'd win $30 or $40 extra. The only problem was my car had broken down and we lived four miles away. But I just got up at four in the morning and jogged to the golf course.

Jesse and Donnie spelled the family name differently because their fathers, who were brothers, never got along when they were young. So Jesse's dad changed the spelling. Jesse and Donnie were barely making it with the club when I came there, having taken it over from the Horizon Corporation, a real estate development outfit based in Tucson. Horizon Hills is located about twenty miles east of El Paso, on Horizon Boulevard off Interstate Highway 10. It's up in the sand hills, a relatively easy course with no trees. It's 7,000 yards, but you could hit a ball 240 yards and it would roll another 100 on that old hard sand. It had been a public course, a place popular with railroaders and Border Patrolmen as well as the well-heeled cotton farmers, but Jesse and Donnie converted it to a private club and were selling memberships for a $25 initiation fee and dues of $12.50 a month.

There was nothing fancy about it: a very small clubhouse located in the corner of an L-shaped motel. We had only twenty battery-operated carts and no shed for them, so we always charged them outside the pro shop. A lot of players brought their bags on pullcarts. I still remember the sound of those pullcarts with the noisy tires when people started showing up to play early. They pulled them across the parking lot to the pro shop: *Squeach, squack, squeach!* I could tell who was pulling each one from the sound of the cart.

Although Jesse was around a lot, Donnie was more involved in the actual management of the club. When we agreed I would work there, he introduced me to Monty Strange, who had heard me talking and laughing in the pro shop. "This is all we need," Monty said. "Another smart-ass Mexican." Well, nobody ever accused Monty of not speaking his mind. We squabbled and cussed and drank a lot in that pro shop but we wound up close friends. Later he worked for me a while as my driver and valet on the tour. Only thing was I carried all the bags.

Life at Horizon Hills was the wildest damn thing in the world. A lot of funny things happened, and a lot of unfunny things.

One day just after I started working there we were drinking beer and arm-wrestling in the bar. Then a couple of friends and I started playing cards with another club member who was the same age as the rest of us.

We're sitting at a table and I started trying to help one of my friends who was drunk and didn't know what was going on. The other club member was dealing, and I told him, "You know, that's not right." And he said, "What's not right?" So I said, "Well, it's not right what you're doing to that guy."

The he made the mistake of standing up.

I hit him with a right cross and he fell over the table. Before he hit the floor I was on top of him. He was bigger than me, maybe about five nine, but he couldn't get up. I was sitting on his back, hitting him in the ears.

Next thing I know my other friend, who was six four and two hundred and thirty pounds, pulled me off. The other guy jumped up and somebody was holding him. We're screaming at each other. "You're cheating him!" I yelled. I didn't know that for sure, but the thing just didn't look right. My drunk friend, who's about my size, said, "No, no, no." And next thing I know he hits me! And I'm taking up for the guy!

"Don't hold me," I told my big friend. So he let me go and I laid my drunk friend out. Then the other guy and I go at it again. We went through a screen door and onto a patio. Then they separated us again.

My big friend got me cornered and said, "Now don't worry—" But I'm still hot. "Get out of my way," I told him, "and don't ever hold me again."

"No, wait a minute," he said and reached for me again. Well, I nailed him with a right cross that should have knocked a tree down. He didn't blink. I hit him again. Same thing. Then he said, "Hey, *hermano* [brother], don't hit me again because you're gonna make me mad."

That's when I realized what was happening and calmed down. I patted my big friend on the arm and said, "Well, come on in and let's have a beer."

The other guy and I both were scratched up a little, and when his wife found out about it, she picked up their golf bags the next day and quit the club. One of the saddest moments of my life was when Donnie called me in to explain what happened. "Well," he said, "just make sure it doesn't happen again." That was one hell of an introduction.

But we had some great games with those cotton farmers swarming all over the course at Horizon Hills, their pockets stuffed with money. Sometimes you'd see a $100 bill blown against a tree and a gang of them would be hurrying down the fairway. We played with six, seven and eight in a group a lot of times but we played fast. They came out there to play 36 or 45 holes a day.

They wouldn't even pay any attention to my little $2 and $5 bets. We'd go into the bar and settle up, and I'd just sit there while Martin Lettunich, Gene Fisher, Leo Collins, Gene McCardle and those guys counted out $50 and $100 bills. Then somebody would say, "Okay, *chico*, how much did I lose to you today?" I'd get $15 from one, $10 from another, $5 from another and go home happy. They would, too.

I never saw anyone carry a gun for protection. Jesse did keep a shotgun in his bag but he used it to kill snakes.

Some days a real Southwester would blow in. That's one helluva wind and sand storm that blows so hard it hurts to be outside. We'd play a couple of more holes and then everyone went to the bar except me. I'd put on a pair of scuba-diving goggles and stay out until dark, hitting 1-irons against the wind and wedges downwind. Mike Doble, who was a good golfer and may have had ideas about the tour himself, said he watched me through the window of the bar one afternoon and decided he should sell hamburgers. Today he has one of the most successful restaurants in El Paso.

These guys confined their drinking to the bar but we had four guys who loved to booze it up while they played. They'd drink maybe five martinis each before they teed off. Then they drank all around the course and drank some more; then they came in. They'd get bombed; four of the funniest guys I ever met.

They never could play in a tournament because they were always drinking, so we came up with a special tournament for them. We called it the Holiday Open, and they loved it. They came all dressed alike—white shirts, knickers, knee stockings and those little French hats with the little balls on top . . . berets. Two gals dressed in gold tights drove their booze cart around the course, and it took them about seven hours to finish. We told the other players, "They're just having fun. Go around them." They came in drunker than skunks and no one had broken 100. We awarded four identical trophies, all inscribed "Winner, Holiday Open." And one of them had a tire mark up his back. He fell down in the middle of the fairway swinging at his ball and another guy ran over him with a cart.

After Donnie saw I was sincere about my work at the club, he gave us an opportunity to move out of the trailer house on the Sparks ranch and into the motel at the course. He gave us two connecting bedrooms with kitchenettes, so we had a little apartment.

"I won't charge you any rent," he said. "All I want is half of any money you make from giving lessons in the afternoon."

Actually, Donnie was testing me to see if I would keep giving lessons or ignore them. I wasn't committed to giving any lessons, but I would come in from playing at five and give lessons until dark. I thought it was decent of him to give me housing at the club so I wanted to be fair with him.

Things were picking up. Bill Eschenbrenner had told me to fill out a new application to the PGA for a Class A card and give it to him. I did, listing as credit references Sears, Zale's Jewelers and SOS Television. He read all the fine print in the PGA constitution and found a way to get around Hardy's refusal to sign as my employer for four years in Dallas. It said that if a chapter official verified my work I could get credit. Bill took it to George Alexander, president of the North Texas chapter, and he verified it. Then he checked with the Southwestern headquarters in Phoenix and was told I could get a Class A card in May of 1967 after earning some credit for my work at Horizon Hills.

I still had a year to go and Bill encouraged me to play in as many local tournaments as possible. I also qualified for the U.S. Open at Olympic in San Francisco in June of 1966. I finished 54th. That didn't do much for me, but playing in all those matches around El Paso did.

Martin Lettunich and Gene McCardle trained me to get ready for them. I played from the blue tees and they'd play from the ladies' tees and they kept the pressure on. They both were 8-handicappers and I'd play their best ball. We'd play for $10 to $25 a man, automatic one-down presses. If I didn't shoot under 66, I'd lose.

Other days we'd play a $5 Nassau—betting $5 on the front nine, $5 on the back nine and $5 on the match—and work on my short game. I had to miss every green with my second shot, then chip it. You think that isn't a helluva practice round? I wasn't wasting any time out there.

One of the toughest matches I ever played was against Bill Eschenbrenner and Frank Redman at Coronado, where I shot 62 and still lost to their best ball. We came up with all types of games. We had the $5 Bogey Game. If four guys were playing and one bogeyed the first hole, that guy then had to pay every other player $5 a hole until each one bogeyed a hole, ending his part of the bet. Once I played for almost two weeks without a bogey.

In the summer of 1966, after I had played that U.S. Open at Olympic, one of the funniest things happened at Horizon Hills. I was in the pro shop one afternoon and the coach of the Clint High School golf team, a guy named Mark Smith, Sr., came in real excited. "Hey, Lee, Gene Littler is in the bar, giving my kids autographs, having a few drinks and telling some great stories!"

I knew that wasn't right because Gene Littler's never taken a drink in his life, he doesn't go to bars and he's never going to tell any stories. "Mark, you gotta be joking," I said.

He said, "I guarantee you it's him. Go look for yourself." I walked to the door, looked at the guy across the room and came back. "That ain't Gene Littler," I said.

"The hell it ain't!" Mark said. "He's already bought three or four rounds of drinks."

Well, the drinking and storytelling went on for two hours, and then this guy called for the bill, which was about $150. "I'll be right back," he told everyone. "I've got to get my wallet out of my car." So they all sat there talking and the next thing they saw was that car going down Horizon Boulevard. That was the last they saw of "Gene Littler."

We did have some genuine celebrities drop in as the months passed, however. Titanic Thompson was one. Raymond Floyd was another. We had a great time with both of them.

I'll never forget that morning when Ti stepped out of his taxi in front of the clubhouse. As he squinted his eyes in the desert sun he looked like an aging Clint Eastwood. Clint made a movie once called *A Fistful of Dollars.* That pretty well fit Ti's line of work, too. He was a legendary hustler and gambler, and I'm sure he had heard at Tenison Park about those cotton farmers at Horizon Hills who loved to bet big money. He came to El Paso to check them out.

Ti was tall and slim, an easy-going type with an ol' Texas drawl. He fit in with the atmosphere at Horizon Hills real well and immediately joined the club. But after a week he had robbed our members of so much money at everything— pitching at the line, blackjack, poker, playing golf right- and left-handed—that they asked him real nice if he would leave.

Man, that was one helluva week!

We even had a call from the Texas Rangers, saying they knew Titanic Thompson was at the club and that we had poker games and other gambling going all night long. Under Texas law at that time any place that sold liquor had to close at midnight, but even if we cut the liquor off we still had guys there until eight o'clock in the morning. The Rangers told us to stop it or they would have to shut us down.

If you saw Ti once, you'd always remember him. He had the youngest pair of hands and clearest blue eyes I ever saw. He was probably close to seventy years old then, but his long, slender hands looked like they belonged to someone twenty-three or twenty-four years old. And his eyes were so clear and young. Maybe it was because he never exposed them to much sun.

I never saw Ti drive a car. He always came out to the club in a taxi and he left in a taxi. I never saw him take a drink and I never saw him smoke. His reflexes were better than most guys' and he could see what was going on. He did everything possible to ensure himself of having the edge in anything he bet on, and he wanted at least to be sure he went into anything even.

One night during a poker game Ti was looking at his cards and someone was speaking Spanish. Ti put his cards down and said, "Gentlemen, I want to tell you now before this gets out of hand. We're speaking only English in this room." There were a lot of people lined up around the walls and Ti wasn't going to risk being at a disadvantage.

He didn't play that much golf in his older days but he did get out on the course at Horizon Hills. One day he was playing a guy for a little money, and I went out and joined them on the ninth hole. Ti was playing left-handed and he said, "C'mon, pro, you want to play this hole?"

"Yeah," I said, "but I don't have any clubs."

"There's mine," Ti said, nodding at his left-handed clubs.

"What do you want to bet?" I asked.

"I'll bet you five dollars on this hole," Ti told me. It was a par-4, water on the right. So I hit his 3-wood left-handed. I hit his 5-iron on the green, two-putted for a par and I beat him.

"Here's your five dollars," Ti said. "You're a goddamn freak."

Ti never beat me out of a nickel because I wouldn't play any of his games. I used his clubs and beat him playing my game, which I had had a little experience with left-handed.

He liked my style. One morning he got me off in a corner at breakfast and offered me a deal as his partner.

"Forget the PGA tour," he told me. "There's no money in it." I believe Ti was thinking about the thirties, forties and early fifties, and how hard it was to make a living out there then. I don't think he could comprehend what was happening with the tour and how commercial it was becoming and how much money a good golfer could make.

He said, "Why don't you just travel the country with me? You play golf and I'll do the betting." It sounded very inviting, but I had this dream of going on the tour and becoming one of the world's top players.

There are many stories about Ti but I don't know how true they are.

He figured everything has a trick to it. The best one I ever heard was about Ti beating a guy out of $5,000 in New York back in the thirties. He took a top hat, set it upside down on the floor of the sitting room in a hotel suite, then stepped into the connecting room and closed the door. There was about an inch clearance above the floor, and he bet the guy he could take a deck of cards and put a dozen of the fifty-two cards into the top hat by flipping them under the door.

Ti put seventeen in the hat, and the guy never knew how he did it. Ti had a friend in the next room who had been waiting on the fire escape. He slipped into the sitting room, grabbed the cards as they came under the door and put them in the hat. After the first seventeen he went back out on the fire escape, closed the window and returned to his room. Ti still had to flip thirty-five more cards under the door, which gave his partner plenty of time to make his exit.

He made a fortune with little things like that.

You always see highway mileage signs: Dallas 17 miles. Well, Ti would dig the sign up and move it five miles out and then bet people about the distance. He might not do it then. He might wait five years. Then one day he would drive by with some guy and say, "Hey, what does that sign say?" "Seventeen miles." "Hey, I'll bet you it's closer to twenty."

Ti figured there was a fool born every day and he dreamed up things like that to make money off them.

Sometimes it didn't work, of course. I saw Arnold Salinas beat him out of $50 in the Horizon Hills clubhouse, and it involved a game in which Ti always had great success.

With the exception of Bob Rosburg, Ti was the best I've ever seen at flipping a card and making it sail through the air. It's an art and I can't do it. I flip them and the cards go straight down. But Ti could stand fifteen feet from a sliced watermelon and flip cards so they would stick in the melon. Well, Arnold was trying to flip a card over the cigarette machine and couldn't do it when Ti walked by. "Tell you what I'm going to do, cowboy," Ti told him. "I'm going to bet you fifty dollars you can't flip a card over that cigarette machine."

Arnold held up the card. "This card?" he asked.

"Yeah," Ti said.

So Arnold took the card, wadded it into a little ball and flipped it over the machine.

"You run into one of these guys every once in a while," Ti said.

Ti had a trick to making long putts. He would take a garden hose, leave it overnight on a green that had just been watered and then move it the next day. When they mowed the green, it left a trough. You could putt a ball and it would roll right down the trough into the hole. I saw Ti bet a guy he could sink three of five putts from 30 feet, then send the ball right through that trough.

He had researched everything he did and he knew the odds. He knew he could do it before he did it. Besides being a great poker and blackjack player, he made it his business to know all this. He would bet that if he dealt five cards and turned them over there would be a pair in those five cards. Ti had studied the odds. He was interesting, very interesting.

I'm sure he sometimes ran into a guy who could beat him pitching coins at the line but Ti had a good gambler's sense. He'd take his loss and get out instead of doubling his bets. Ti would never do something stupid trying to get even.

I asked him how he got the name Titanic and his answer didn't make sense. He said he was in a bar once, bet a guy he could jump the pool table flat-footed, and when he did it the guy said, "You sank me like the *Titanic.*"

I've also heard he got the nickname because he got off the *Titanic* before it sank. As I understand the history of the *Titanic,* very few men got off, only women and children. I heard he dressed like a woman and got in a lifeboat, but I have no idea how true that is. Maybe somewhere along the line he told somebody he got off the *Titanic* and the story grew from there. Or maybe they called him Titanic simply because he drowned everybody.

Ti died a few years ago and he spent his last days in a rest home. Again, I don't know how true it is, but I heard that by the time Ti died he owned every wheelchair, every crutch and every walking cane there and leased them for a dime and twenty-five cents a week to the man who operated the home. He had won them playing checkers with the old people there.

He was beautiful.

In the fall, a couple of months after Ti's visit, I was working around the clubhouse when Fat Mickey, one of the big money guys from Tenison Park, walked in. Ti had told them about his experience out there in El Paso, and they sent Fat Mickey out as advance man to set up a match for Raymond Floyd.

Raymond was in his early twenties then—a big, blond, good-looking kid with a wonderful touch—and one of the great young players on the tour. He was living in Dallas and he hung out at Tenison when he wasn't on the tour. Raymond really loved those money games.

The most difficult thing in the world is to handicap a pro playing against amateurs, but the guys at Tenison had some exotic methods. They came up with gimmick games for Raymond to play. He would hit two tee shots, then play the worst one.

In this game he'd play a hole by having to play his worst ball twice. If one ball was on the green and the other in the bunker, he had to play two out of the bunker. If one putt went in the hole and one went 20 feet past, he putted two from 20 feet. If he sank one putt and the other went three feet past, he putted two from three feet. I've never seen too many pros who could break 40 for nine holes playing this way.

Raymond also played a lot at Tenison betting his best ball. He'd usually bet he'd score about 62 or 63. He'd do it sometimes, but he lost more than he won. It was just something to do and Raymond liked the action. He was a bachelor then and he lived fast. He was game for anything, just the kind everyone at Tenison liked.

Fat Mickey was a gambler and sort of a small-time bookmaker. He died a few years ago, and the story was that he dropped dead in a dice game in West Texas when he got very excited and almost got in a fight. But the day he walked up to me he still was very much alive and had a big smile on his face.

He said, "Hey, these farmers out here like to play golf, don't they?"

"Yeah," I told him.

"They sure like the way you play, don't they?"

"Yeah."

"They'll bet on you, too, won't they?"

"Yeah."

"You think they'd bet on you if we brought Raymond Floyd out here to play?"

"Yeah, if we played my home course."

I got real interested then because the toughest thing in the world is to play a professional on his home course if he's a good player. He knows all the right clubs to use. He knows every blade of grass. He knows every break in the greens. He knows the texture of the sand. And desert greens are the toughest to putt on simply because there is no consistent way the greens will break. If you're playing on an ocean course, everything goes toward the ocean. If you're playing in a mountain region, you look for the highest mountain and everything breaks away from that. But in flat desert a putt on one hole will break east, the one on the next hole will break south and the next will break west. I liked my chances against Raymond Floyd.

Fat Mickey stayed that night and talked to Martin Lettunich, Gene Fisher and some other guys. He played some poker and lost a few dollars to them. It was strictly a setup. He thought he had found a gravy train. Martin told him, "Yeah, bring the boy out. We'll arrange something."

So two days later Raymond Floyd drove up. I'd never met Raymond and I got a cart and went out to pick up his golf bag. I carried his clubs into the locker room, put them in a locker, brushed his shoes, cleaned them and polished them.

Raymond asked me, "Well, who am I supposed to play?" "Me," I said. He looked at me. "You? What do you do?" I said, "Well, I'm a combination everything. I'm the cart man, shoe man, clubhouse man and pro."

He gave me a funny look and then he went in to have breakfast with Fat Mickey and some other guys from Tenison.

"What time do we play?" he asked.

"One o'clock," Fat Mickey told him. "You wanna go look at the course?"

Raymond said, "Naw, I'm playing this boy here. I don't need to go look at any golf course."

Raymond put down some of his money, too, and the betting must have gotten pretty heavy. I know those cotton farmers tossed $100 bills around like most people treat dollar bills and they wanted to bet more on me than the Tenison crowd could cover. I really was under pressure.

It was the funniest sight in the world when Raymond and I teed off. There were a bunch of pickup trucks bouncing down the fairway, full of guys drinking beer and watching our match.

Well, the first round I was really hot. Raymond shot 67, but I shot 65. When we finished there was still a lot of daylight. Raymond said, "Let's go another nine." I said no and he got mad. I told him, "Look, I can't play another nine. I've got to put the carts up, clean the clubs and all that stuff." He said, "I can't believe this. Here I am playing a cart man, a bag-storage man, and I can't beat him."

So he went into the lounge and started playing cards. Raymond was really kind of a wild man then, restless for action. Two of the Horizon members talked him into going dove hunting and they took off in a pickup with some shotguns. They hunted till sundown, drank a lot of beer and didn't shoot a single damn dove.

The next day Raymond told me, "I ain't never going dove hunting with those crazy bastards again."

"What's the matter?" I asked.

"They shoot at everything," he said. "We were sitting on the ground and there weren't any doves around and I had my hat about two feet from me. One guy said, 'Aw, hell, there are no doves. Let's shoot something.' And he shot my hat!"

Now Raymond was not one to go someplace and not try something. So when it got dark the guys said, "Hey, let's go to Juárez and have some fun." I don't know if they did it purposely to get him all screwed up for the next day's match, but Raymond said, "Let's go." So they put up the shotguns, drove over to Juárez and started hitting the bars.

They stayed in Juárez all night but Raymond came out the next day ready to play. By now word had gotten around that Raymond Floyd was at Horizon Hills and the crowd picked up. Everybody made the same bets and we teed off. I shot 65 again and he shot 66. Again he wanted to play another nine, and I couldn't play because I had to put those damn carts up. So he went in and played blackjack again.

I didn't know how long Raymond was going to stay, but he came out a third day and beat me on the front nine. He shot 31 and some of the guys pressed on the back nine, trying to make their money back. I'll never forget the final hole. I had an 8-foot eagle putt, he had a 6-foot birdie putt, and if I made my eagle and he missed his birdie, I would beat him for the third straight day.

But I missed and Raymond won the round. That's when he got his clubs, shook my hand and said, "I can find mu-u-uch easier games than this. I have had enough."

Since that day Raymond has won a lot of money and a lot of tournaments, including the PGA twice and the Masters. But people still ask him, "Did you ever go to El Paso?"

"I sure did," he says, "and let me tell you something. If I hadn't left there when I did, they would have had to send me home C.O.D."

6.
Jersey Bounce

My wife came up with a couple of new things during that first year I worked at Horizon Hills. First, she was nicknamed Clyde because Donnie Whittington's wife also is named Claudia. Second, she decided to enter me in the 1967 U.S. Open without telling me.

That turned out to be a helluva good idea.

My first U.S. Open in 1966 at Olympic, the place Billy Casper beat Arnold Palmer in an 18-hole playoff, wasn't one of my all-time thrills. I shot 303 for 72 holes, tied for 54th and won $600. I didn't leave my heart in San Francisco. The only fun I had was congratulating Rives McBee, an old buddy from Garland, when he shot 64 in the second round to tie the 18-hole record for the championship.

I'd never played a great golf course like Olympic, a course with that kind of rough. I'd never hit a ball out of tall grass before. I had played municipal courses all my life and they didn't have rough. Or bunkers.

The first time I got in the rough at Olympic I didn't have

any idea what to do with it. I wasn't any good hitting out of tall rough because of my flat swing. I started watching guys to see how they got out of that rough. Don January has always amazed me. He's very good out of tall rough because his swing is so upright and he reaches the ball without hitting much grass. He takes the club straight up and he drops it on the ball. So does Jack Nicklaus.

Over the years I've learned a little bit about playing out of the rough, and fortunately I've been able to avoid it—probably more than others. But at Olympic I couldn't get it out of the rough and I decided if that was what the U.S. Open was like I wasn't going to mess with it too much.

The next year when the USGA sent me the entry blank for Baltusrol, I wasn't interested. I just tossed it aside. We were scraping for money, but Clyde got the entry fee of $20 together and sent it in. When the USGA accepted me and sent me more information I didn't want to fool with trying to qualify again, but I did.

Local qualifying was played in Odessa, about 300 miles from El Paso. I shot 134 for 36 holes, which was lowest in the nation. So I went to the sectional qualifying at Great Southwest Club, near Dallas. I finished second, won $200 and a place in the U.S. Open. I took my money and went back to El Paso, wondering how I could get to Springfield, New Jersey.

Well, Jesse and Donnie were excited that I was going. They cleaned out every cash register at the club and gave me $400. So I bought an airline ticket and started packing. That didn't take long. I had six shirts, three pairs of slacks and one pair of golf shoes. I only had twelve clubs in my golf bag. I never carried a 1-iron or 2-iron then, simply because I couldn't hit any decent shots with them.

When I walked off the plane in Newark I didn't even know where I was going to stay that week. I got into a taxi in front of the airport and asked the driver for some help. He looked me over and figured out I wasn't one of the Rockefellers, so he took me to a little place on Highway 22 called the Union Motel.

It was strictly small budget, but to me it looked pretty fancy. When you grow up with dirt floors, no plumbing and no electricity, any room that has a television, lights and hot and cold running water is paradise. And the place had a coin laundry. I could take twenty-five cents and wash everything I had.

Naturally, none of the big-name golfers were staying at the Union Motel but I met another Mexican-American who was also in the U.S. Open. Cesar Sanudo, a young pro from California, had played college golf at Lamar University in Texas and we hit it off great. We played our practice rounds together and we felt a little more at home, knowing each other.

It was my first trip east of the Mississippi River and I didn't have a sports coat or a suit. You had to wear a coat nearly everywhere you went to eat, so I walked about a mile up Highway 22 over a bridge and ate dinner every night at a Chinese restaurant. It was the only place I found where I could go in without a coat.

It was raining some of the time, so I took my umbrella and sloshed along. I'd get muddy from cars splashing in chuckholes. Then I'd reach the restaurant, eat dinner, drink about ten beers and have a helluva time getting back to my room. I'm lucky I wasn't killed. They told me Highway 22 was one of the most dangerous roads in New Jersey. Only trouble was, when I got back to my room I was always starving.

Baltusrol is one of the famous old clubs in the East, with one of those big brick Tudor clubhouses sitting up on a hillside. I'd never seen anything like it and I was nervous about just going inside. The first morning I had to borrow a jacket to enter the dining room. After that I said to hell with breakfast and I did without.

But I loved it out on the course. I showed up on Sunday, played four practice rounds and shot 280, which usually will

win an Open. This was a legitimate 280. I was scared to death
and put down my actual score even for practice.

I saw a sign at the first tee: "Play one ball only." I cracked
to the officials, "The first time I played in the U.S. Open I
lost my ball on the 12th hole so I quit. What if I lose my ball
here?" They laughed and said, "Aw, you can play another
one." That's how scared I was.

After my last practice round I called home. "I can't believe
I shot 280," I told Clyde. "This golf course is just gorgeous.
It's long but I love it because it's in such great condition."
I hadn't seen a tumbleweed blow across the fairway all week.

I was beginning to feel more comfortable around Baltusrol. I even made a couple of good friends there.

One was Chuck Smith, who owned a nearby Cadillac
agency and was married to one of the singing Fontaine Sisters. I met him one afternoon early in the week and he invited
me to sit with him and drink a beer. He ordered me another
and another and then he said, "Tell you what: You drink 'em
and I'll pay for 'em." He didn't know what he was letting
himself in for. Every day I met him on the patio and sometimes I'd drink fifteen.

We'd sit there and talk and it was very pleasant. Then no
one knew me. No one bothered me. No one cared. As far as
they knew, I was Chuck Smith's gardener.

The other new friend was Jack Duffy, my caddie. He was
an Irishman in his forties and he really knew golf. Those
caddies up there prided themselves in being the best. He drew
my name and I'm sure he wondered, "Who in the hell is
this?" But as he watched me play he warmed up to me.

The first practice round he was lagging about twenty paces
behind me the whole way. I shot 68 and the next day we came
out and he was about ten paces behind me and I shot 70.
Before I finished practicing he was way out in front of me.
"Kid, to hell with Nicklaus and Palmer and the rest of 'em,"
he told me. "You can hit this ball."

I still felt nervous stepping on that famous old course for

the first round but I also felt confident, because I had played so well in practice. I was anxious to see how I could score when it counted.

Well, I shot 72 in the first round, followed that with a 70 and 71. So after three rounds I had 213 and was just three shots behind the leaders—Nicklaus, Palmer and Casper.

The USGA had continuous putting in the Open that year, trying to speed up play. The rule was if you weren't stepping in someone else's line you had to keep putting. It wasn't a problem the first three rounds but it bothered me the last day.

I birdied the 11th or 12th hole and they put my name on the leader board, the first time I'd ever seen my name up there. Everybody thought I was Italian. Trevino in Italian means three wines, and it seemed to me we were in the Italian capital of the world. So my gallery started getting bigger and bigger and the suits darker and darker. By the 18th, even the Godfather was there.

I was playing with Dave Hill, and on the 14th I rolled a 20-foot putt up there about eighteen inches from the cup. It looked like I could finish and then it looked questionable about where his marker was. I tried to straddle his marker and putt out even though Dave told me, "Mark your ball. You don't have to putt again." I was scared the USGA was going to say something so I went ahead. I missed and 3-putted. Then I went right to 15 and 3-putted it.

I parred 16, 17 and 18 and finished with a 70 and 283. Nicklaus shot 65 to win by four with 275, but I won more money than I'd ever had in my life: $6,000. If I hadn't 3-putted 14 and 15 I would have tied with January for third at 281, two shots behind Palmer and one ahead of Casper, and my prize money would have been $8,750.

I wasn't complaining, though. I rushed into the clubhouse and called Clyde.

"I'm not believing this," I told her. "I just won $6,000!"

"Hey," she said, "I did all right with my twenty dollars."

We talked a little longer but I'm not sure what we said.

We were kind of emotional. After I hung up the phone, I remembered how hot and thirsty I was. I joined Chuck Smith on the patio and started drinking beer. I wanted to hang around and find out about my check. Hell, I was the richest Mexican in the world.

After a while I learned they were sending my check home, but I stuck around. I was the last one to leave the club that night. The tournament was over and Chuck Smith and I were still sitting on the patio, getting soused. And that night, just like all week, no one spoke to me or asked me for my autograph. That shows you how much I was known.

My caddie, Jack Duffy, was delighted I played so well, of course. After we finished that Sunday I gave him all the money I had with the exception of $20. I gave him about $125 and I told him as soon as I cashed the check I'd send him the rest of his money. "No problem," he said. When I got home I sent him another $600.

But first I made another stop. After the final round, Steve Shabala of the tour staff asked me, "Do you want to go to Cleveland?"

"What's in Cleveland?" I asked.

"Our next tournament," he said. "They're holding a spot for you in the field if you want to play. Are you a member of the PGA?"

"Sure," I told him. I had gotten my Class A card six weeks before.

I told him I would play in Cleveland, and I changed my airline ticket. But when I got there I didn't have a room and I had five bucks in my pocket. Fortunately, I could check into a motel without paying in advance, but I couldn't enter the tournament until Clyde flew in there Wednesday and brought me $50 to pay the entry fee. When Clyde arrived she said everyone was excited in El Paso about my finishing fifth, and after she told me that, I wanted to go home and be the hero.

Ken Still was paired with me the first two rounds at Cleveland, and he still tells the story about what I did to get out of there. I was really playing up a storm, and on Friday I came to the 16th hole at Aurora—a par-5, dogleg left—and I asked somebody what was going to make the cut. The guy said something like four over. I was two under at the time, but all I wanted to do was take off and fly to El Paso. So on purpose I took a driver and aimed at a house out-of-bounds right and hit three balls at that house, one right behind the other, to where I'd make a number big enough that I wouldn't make the cut and I could fly home and be with my friends. Ken Still says he never saw a man try to miss a cut purposely by knocking a house down over on the right.

Clyde and I went home and we had a great party at Horizon Hills that Saturday night. Everybody was there. When I walked in, Martin Lettunich came over and threw his big arm around my shoulder.

"Hey, *chico*," he said, "we're sure proud of you."

I'll always enjoy remembering those days at Baltusrol. It was one of those times when my life took a new direction. I only wish everything had gone as well for my friend Cesar Sanudo all these years.

When I called him in San Diego in the spring of 1981 and asked him to come to Dallas for the Byron Nelson Classic, he was feeling pretty low. He hadn't finished higher than 100th on the tour-money list for eight years and he'd won just a little over $6,000 for the entire previous year. He had just missed the cut in New Orleans and he was hesitant about coming to Dallas, even when I told him he didn't have to worry about a place to sleep and eat. He could stay with me.

Well, later he called back and said he was coming. It wasn't until the tournament was over that I learned Cesar didn't have the air fare. He went to this guy in San Diego and made a deal: The guy gave him $500 and Cesar agreed to pay him half of anything he won in the Nelson.

Cesar got off well, shooting a 70 in the first round, then

70 again the next day. He was in the hunt. Then he shot 75 on Saturday. No telling how often he'd been through that before: the buildup, then the letdown.

But on Sunday Cesar went out and shot another 70. I grabbed a phone and called his wife, Jackie, in San Diego.

"Jackie, all that dog of a husband needed to do to finish tenth was double-bogey the eighteenth," I told her. I heard her sigh. "Well, what happened?" she asked me.

"He parred it and finished sixth!" I said. That was worth $10,050.

I heard her drop the phone. Man, I know how she felt. That night I called Clyde from Baltusrol we just cried at both ends of the line.

7.
"Who Is That Guy?"

My success in the 1967 U.S. Open caused me to move up my plans for joining the tour. I thought I would hang around El Paso for a few months, play in the Mexican Open, the New Mexican Open, the Texas State Open and a few local events and start out in January 1968 as a regular tour member. But when I got home I received invitations to the Western Open, the Westchester and the American Golf Classic.

I decided to join the tour six months early, but I wasn't going to travel by commercial airline. Arnold Palmer had a private jet. So did Jack Nicklaus. I got my own ship—a 1965 Plymouth station wagon I bought from Jesse Whittenton for $1,600 on time. We loaded some clothes and my clubs in it and took off. I was pilot, Clyde was navigator and Lesley was the passenger.

As a navigator, Clyde wasn't so hot. We were going to the Minnesota Classic first, since it came the week before the Western. We left El Paso, headed up through Clovis, New

Mexico, across Western Oklahoma and up through Iowa. We got lost so many times it was unbelieveable. I thought we would spend the summer in Iowa. I've never seen so damn much corn in my entire life.

We'd be breezing along the highway and Clyde would look at the map and say, "Turn right here." I'd turn right and she'd say, "No, I want you to turn left right there." So we'd turn around and go back.

We reached Minneapolis–St. Paul on the weekend and found a plain little motel room with a kitchen near the course at Hazeltine. I practiced some and then went out early Monday for the qualifying round. When I shot a 79 I was sure I wouldn't get in the tournament.

I'll never forget my first hole: a dogleg left, par-4. I was so nervous I duck-hooked my tee shot into some hedges and lost my ball. I hit another one and made 6 on the hole. I found out Hazeltine is a mean old golf course. It has four par-5s that are 600 yards long. We played the U.S. Open there in 1970 and that's when Dave Hill blasted it, saying all it needed was some cows and a few acres of corn to be a perfect farm.

When I finished, I started packing my gear to leave when Jack Tuthill of the PGA staff came in the clubhouse. "I shot 79, so I'm going on to Chicago," I told him. "Wait a minute," he said. "People are shooting 80s out there. You'll qualify."

Well, I did, and I made $800 in the tournament. Lou Graham won it and Bob Verwey, Gary Player's brother-in-law, finished second. That seemed strange because he's the shortest hitter in the history of the game and Hazeltine was the longest course.

The Western was played at Beverly, one of the major clubs in the Chicago area. Arnold Palmer lost there to Bob Stanton in a playoff. I made the cut but finished low, and I made only $200. Still, I had $1,000 to show for two weeks so I wasn't sweating the expenses. We stayed in inexpensive motels and gasoline was cheap then. We just kept driving through the Midwest in that Plymouth station wagon. Lesley had just turned two, and she had a rocking-chair duck in the back seat with a potty in it. The other pros kidded about it. "We knew that was Trevino's car going down the road," they said, "because we could see the duck rocking in the back."

What bothered me more than anything was the short day I was spending at the golf course. I was accustomed to making it an eight- or nine-hour job: playing, practicing, putting, chipping. But as soon as I finished a round I felt obligated to rush back and take my wife and daughter to eat or do something because they had been cooped up in the room all day. That caused me to try some strange things.

We went to Akron for the American Golf Classic, and when I came back to the motel after shooting a pretty good first round we decided to polish the car. Then I hit golf balls out of the parking lot and into the trees. You think that wasn't tough, trying to put a tee into that asphalt? I was so sore from polishing the car that I didn't hit the ball well for the next two rounds. I didn't make any money in the tournament, and that's when Clyde said, "This life isn't for me. Why don't you just try to play golf and let me go home with Lesley?"

We drove on to Hartford, I put them on a plane and then I had the time I needed to spend on my game. I won $2,150 in the tournament and felt even better when I met the Z Man.

That's Pete Zaccagnino, a former bomber pilot who became a lawyer and one of the best amateur golfers in New England. The caddies told me I had to meet him because they knew I talked a lot. He and I met on the practice tee and we became great friends. He's about my height—five seven or so —but he doesn't weigh as much. And he does like to talk.

I always remember special people and places. While I was in Hartford I stayed at the Travelers Lodge. It had no restaurant and I had a little bitty room, but the owner took a liking to me and made me feel at home. A few years later, when

I had won a few tournaments and had more money, I went back and took Clyde. "Why are you staying in this place?" she asked me. "I'm comfortable here," I told her.

Expensive rooms and elaborate hotels just don't impress me. I'd still rather have a motel where I can drive right up to the door and go into my room than walk through the lobby of a fancy high-rise hotel. Give me a shower, television, telephone and clean sheets and I don't give a damn if rats are running around the floor as long as they don't climb on the bed.

Having come from a poor background, I never minded needling my friends when they started moaning about living conditions. That first year Chi Chi Rodriguez told me, "For $100 I could have killed a thousand cockroaches between New York and Los Angeles." "You ought to," I said. "You brought a million with you."

When I drove down to New York for the Westchester tournament I had some company. Rives McBee and Dave Eichelberger, two pros from Texas, hitched a ride and so did Ted Makalena, a fine player from Hawaii who became a great friend. They started riding with me on short trips, but when it was a long hop they would fly and I would drive alone. Ted became like a brother to me. He didn't drink so he didn't hit the bars at night, but if I went out and wasn't in my room by ten-thirty he'd come looking for me. We started calling him Ted Papa-Papa Rice, after a TV commercial done by Hawaiians. He called me Mum. "Hey," I said, "that's the name of a deodorant." He laughed. "For you," he said, "it stands for Mixed-Up Mexican."

I couldn't argue with that. When we reached New York I dropped them off at a fancy Westchester motel. I drove across town to a little motel in a black neighborhood. It was the type of place where you paid for your room in advance each day. When I came in from the course I would stop at the office and pay my $8.50 to sleep another night. Then I'd go in the bar and have a few beers. Oh, it was tough! I wouldn't go in there now with a machine gun.

But I walked right in, talked to everybody and never had any problems. The lady who took care of my room was the wife of the owner and she was really nice. I liked to keep fruit juices and milk in my room, so I'd put them in a plastic bag filled with ice and put the bag in a little wastebasket. Every night I'd come home and find everything packed in fresh ice.

Westchester probably was the easiest of all the tour courses I've played. But in its way, it was hard. You had to keep the ball straight and it had smaller, elevated greens. If you missed the greens at Westchester, you had trouble getting it up and down. I had a good week there, even if I had two 67s rained out.

I was paired with Gene Sarazen the first 36 holes and he was a grand old man. He was very nice to me. After I shot that second 67, he told the press, "I just played with a man that you're going to hear a lot about. He's an up-and-coming star and he's going to win a lot of golf tournaments."

Nicklaus won Westchester, but I made my share of birdies and tied for seventh. That tournament had the biggest prize money on the tour at the time and I collected $8,100. So for the five tournaments since I left El Paso I had won $11,200. "Geez," I said to myself, "how long has this been going on?"

Westchester is also where I met two of the best friends I've ever had, John Homorsky and Joe Iazzi. John was a tool-and-die maker and Joe an old Navy man who worked for the Post Office. They came down from Connecticut to see the tournament and we started talking and drank a few beers. We went to dinner a couple of nights and they took me to Italian restaurants because everyone up there still thought I was Italian. I never ate so much spaghetti and veal in my life. We still get together every year, but unfortunately some people think they're hangers-on. Not these guys. They've paid their own way and given me a lot more than they've received.

Joe is from New Canaan, Connecticut, the area that Sarazen, Tony Manero and Julius Boros came from, and after he met me, he told his old cronies, "I just watched a kid named Lee Trevino play who's gonna make people forget Ben Hogan." Well, I didn't make them forget Hogan but I have proved I can play. Joe's always been proud as a peacock that he saw me play once and predicted I was going to be that good.

In Toronto that summer we played the Canadian Open on the Board of Trade course designed by Trent Jones and it was really mean. The greens were 10,000 square feet with double undulations. I putted the ball from the back of the green and it disappeared twice, going through those valleys. I led after the second round, but Billy Casper eventually won the tournament. I finished fourth and won $4,300. By then I knew I belonged out there.

Then we played the Hawaiian Open in the fall and it was a pleasure to be there because Ted Makalena was defending champion. I finished in the money, like I did in all but one of the thirteen tournaments I played after joining the tour. I ended up winning $26,472, and was voted Rookie of the Year. I finished 45th on the money list which meant that I got a top-60 exemption from qualifying for tour events in 1968. Then I won the U.S. Open and got a lifetime exemption. The Minnesota Classic turned out to be the only tour event where I had to qualify.

In December of 1967 it was time to split the money I had won. The agreement with Jesse Whittenton and Don Whittington had been that they would sponsor me that year and I would receive 60 percent of the money I won after expenses. They only put up $400 to send me to the U.S. Open and never had to reach in their pockets again, but they were sincere and I wanted to do right by them.

They didn't try to hustle me. We went to the bank and Donnie said, "Here's your money." Suddenly I had $17,000 in my hand!

"What am I going to do with this?" I asked.

"I don't know," Donnie said, "unless you'd like to be a third partner in the golf course."

They had been running Horizon Hills for a year and a half and invested $12,000 each in it. Donnie offered me a third partnership for $12,000 and I gave him the money. The club was popular and growing and I liked the place. It was a good investment. When we sold it back to the Horizon Land Corporation a couple of years later we got $86,000 for it.

That one investment could have ended my business dealings with Donnie and Jesse. We had no agreement for 1968. I could have walked out, gone back to Dallas and never seen them again. But because they gave me my start I felt it was only right to include them as partners in everything I did.

But I made a mistake when we sat down with the lawyer to draw up an agreement.

"How long do you want them as partners?" he asked me.

I wasn't business-minded and didn't know what I was doing, so I told him, "Indefinitely."

Years later I really regretted that.

The first six months of 1968 were a special time in my life. I remember two unusual car trips. One took me past huge snowbanks in Northern Arizona on my way to a tournament I couldn't play in, the other through upstate New York on a warm June day as I headed for my first victory on the tour.

I was sick with the flu when I left for the first tournament of the year in January, the Bing Crosby in Pebble Beach, California, but I drove all the way alone in a new Chevrolet I had leased for the tour. It had a big stereo set and I had some eight-track cassettes of the Tijuana Brass playing as I headed out through Albuquerque and Flagstaff, Arizona.

I took the northern route to California because I wanted to see a lot of snow, having never seen much all my years in Dallas. I wasn't disappointed. I was lucky I didn't get killed driving through Flagstaff. The snowplows had piled snow nine feet high on both sides of the road and it was like driving in a refrigerator. People had flags on their cars so you could see others coming into an intersection. After all of that, it was nice to reach the Monterey Peninsula and see the Pacific Ocean, even if I was sick.

I played some practice rounds, then withdrew from the tournament and stayed in my room for two days. The caddies took care of me because I was staying in the same shabby little motel where most of them were. I had a 102-degree temperature, so they called a doctor to come by and give me a shot. When I was well enough I packed up and left.

Some start for the year.

I didn't even get to meet Bing. But I had that pleasure in later years. He always walked around the course with his cane, smoking a pipe and wearing his knickers, saying hello to the players. He was one of the greatest things that ever happened to golf.

But by the time I headed for Rochester and the U.S. Open at Oak Hill in June, I had some momentum. I had finished second in my last two tournaments at Houston and Atlanta and I felt I was at the top of my game. As I passed through Utica, New York, I saw some kids playing baseball in a park so I stopped, got myself a Coke and a hamburger and watched the whole game. I had been in Stamford, Connecticut, practicing for a few days and I was in no hurry. I stopped several times, just to enjoy a ball game or the scenery. It's a ten-hour drive but it took me two days.

I had come very close to winning my first tour title in my home state. I led the Houston Open at Champions with two holes to go, but I was really nervous. I was playing with Roberto de Vicenzo, the fine player from Argentina who had lost a shot at the Masters championship a few weeks earlier when a scorecard error kept him from a playoff with Bob Goalby. I caused my downfall on the 16th hole, a par-3 with the pin over the bunker on the left, when I hit a 4-iron eight feet from the hole but missed the putt that would have given me a two-shot lead on Roberto. The two closing holes at Champions are difficult. I bogeyed the 17th, a long hole with a lake on the left, and Roberto parred to tie me. Then on 18, I shanked a 3-iron from the middle of the fairway and my ball almost went on the driving range. From there I putted the ball to three feet from the hole, but I missed the next one and Roberto won by a shot.

I shook hands with him and he looked at me with those big, soft eyes. In his broken English he said, "I thank you very much. You are young and you win many tournaments. I am old and maybe never have another chance to win one." I didn't feel all that bad, finishing second.

When I came in second again at Atlanta, it bothered me more. I shot a 74 the first round and I was solid hot when I walked off the 18th green. Clyde was standing there and she asked me a question, but I paid no attention to her. I hit a rope on the gate and it flew up and hit her in the eyes. It was a terrible, stupid thing for me to do. I felt so bad that I told her, "I'm going to win this tournament for you." I came close. I shot the next three rounds in the 60s, but Bob Lunn still beat me by two shots.

After spending some time practicing with my pals Joe Iazzi and John Homorsky in Connecticut, I felt relaxed and confident when I reached Rochester. I'd never been there, but I'd heard about Oak Hill, one of the top courses in America. It just turned out to be one of those weeks when everything went right.

To begin with, I stayed in the home of a family I hadn't met. I hadn't tried that before because I have my own way of relaxing away from the course. If I'm in a motel room I like to lie in bed and watch television or hit balls on the carpet until one or two o'clock in the morning. But when Paul Kircher wrote and told me his kids had picked me as the player they wanted to stay in their home during U.S. Open week, I accepted. With all those people around, I figured I'd always have somebody to talk to.

Paul had been a pitcher in the New York Yankees' farm system and was a good amateur golfer. He had done well in the insurance business in Rochester and he and Barbara had five children then. They have seven now. They're a sweetheart of a family—Catholic and very religious.

They really knew nothing about me when they decided to invite me. Paul said later they picked me because I was new on the tour and they thought I might need some help with my expenses. They didn't even know if I could speak English.

When Paul took me to their home it was a hot afternoon and Barbara was wearing a black bathing suit like she was going swimming. Paul said, "Don't mind Barb. She dresses like this all the time." She was a very attractive lady and I couldn't help looking at her, walking around the house in a bathing suit.

Then I saw what she was doing in the kitchen. She was unpacking a whole box of canned Mexican food she ordered from El Paso. I told her I really didn't like Mexican food that much unless it was homemade and that I just liked some grapefruit and a little toast and bacon in the morning. I'm sure she still has that box of Mexican food to this day.

Maybe it was because the Kirchers made me feel comfortable at home that I felt so good at Oak Hill. I played practice rounds with Doug Sanders, who was one of the best players of the time. I was driving the ball extremely well and my putting was really good. I was using an old Tommy Armour putter with a gooseneck that my friend Dennis Lavender, the pro at Cedar Crest municipal course in Dallas, had fixed up for me a few weeks before when I was playing the Byron Nelson Classic. I'll never forget his words: "I'm going to fix you a putter you can win the Open with."

I was paired with Deane Beman and Gay Brewer the first two rounds and shot 69–68 to go three under par. Oak Hill was a very difficult course but I was splitting every fairway with my tee shots. My chipping and putting were strong. I had my game under control. Still, I didn't know if I had a chance to win.

Brewer was the real star in our threesome because he had won the Masters in 1967 and was another of the top players of that era. He had that perfect loop in his swing, which is a lot better than trying to take the club straight back and then bring it straight ahead to the ball. That's like trying to walk a straight line when you're drunk.

Beman had tremendous courage and an exceptional short game, but he was small and didn't have the strength to hit the ball well out of the rough. He had to lay up and sacrifice shots. If he'd had the strength of players like Nicklaus, Palmer, Player, Tom Watson or me, he never would have become the commissioner of golf. He'd be one of the superstars of the game.

But I was the one who was hot, and after two rounds I was second in the field, one shot behind Bert Yancey. We played together in the third round on Saturday and I shot 69 but Bert had 68, so he led by two when we teed off on Sunday. I was really pumped up. I knew that I was the underdog and that nobody expected me to win. We had a gallery following us, but there was a much bigger gallery behind us. The USGA had Palmer, who was almost in last place in the tournament, in the final twosome that day.

It's customary for players with high scores to tee off early in the round, but they changed it at Oak Hill because Palmer was so popular. That probably would bother me today because that big gallery walks up on you when you're putting. But I didn't pay any attention to it then.

I was wearing a red shirt, red socks and black pants that day, and for a long time after that it was traditional for me to wear those colors on Sunday. I called them my payday colors and I made them so popular that a lot of my gallery wore black and red on Sunday. Later I won the Chrysler tournament in Sydney, Australia, and received a new car, which I gave my mother-in-law. She asked for a black and red one and named it Payday.

But that day I was still just an unknown golfer who was dressed kinda strange. Palmer was playing right behind me and Nicklaus just ahead. A few times one of them gave me a puzzled look. It was like Butch Cassidy and the Sundance Kid watching that railroad detective who tracked them across the country and asking themselves, "Who is that guy?"

I believe that in his heart Yancey thought he had it won because I was the only person giving him any heat. Nicklaus was five shots behind me. But Yancey didn't know my outlook on life, and how I always had been an underdog. I knew I could shoot 80 and nobody would be surprised, but if I played well, it put pressure on Yancey, who was expected to win. I liked my position but I was still mighty nervous when we teed off.

I hit a low screamer and the ball barely got over the rough and onto the fairway. I took a bogey and I'm sure Yancey never dreamed I would play the next 17 holes two under par.

He didn't play well that day, but you couldn't tell it by watching him move around the course. He had gone to school at West Point and he always looked the same out there, a military man who walked down the fairway like he was marching. He was self-disciplined, a tall blond guy with a beautiful swing that made him the Gene Littler of that era—a machine. He also reminded me a lot of Don January . . . never in a hurry. He had one flow. Not so with myself. I get excited and I get a little fast.

Yancey's downfall came on 11, 12 and 13. I birdied the first two and he 3-putted 13, a par-5 that I also birdied with a 6-foot putt. That blew it open. I went to 14 with a 5-shot lead and all I wanted to do was finish. I parred that hole and then on 15, a relatively short hole, I hit the flag with an 8-iron. I'll never forget that because I asked my caddie, a kid named

Kevin Quinn, "What do you think I ought to hit here?" "Five-iron," he said. And I said, "Man, you've got to be joking. My caddie's choking worse than I am."

As it was, an 8-iron was too much club. The ball bounced 15 feet from the hole but I 2-putted for a par. On 16 I made a nervous 7-footer for par, and then on 17 I hit the ball with my old Tommy Armour gooseneck and sank a 20-footer for a par after chipping up short. On 18, I missed the fairway to the left and when I wanted to get it out of the rough and back into the fairway with a sand wedge, my caddie wouldn't let me.

"You don't want to be remembered as the U.S. Open champion who laid up on the last hole," he said.

I took a 6-iron but I couldn't get the ball out of the rough, and I lost a stroke. I was solid hot so I took a sand wedge and took the hardest swing I could. The pin was set right by the bunker and I was aiming at the right of the center of the green just to get it on the green. The ball came out of that tall grass, went straight at the flag and stopped two feet from the hole. Then I realized if I made the putt I'd be the first man in history to shoot four rounds in the 60s in the U.S. Open. I made it. I had another 69 and won by four shots over Nicklaus, who had shot 66 to beat Yancey out of second place.

My 275 for 72 holes also tied the record set by Nicklaus at Baltusrol the year before, one that stood until Jack went back there and won the 1980 U.S. Open with 272. Nobody could say I backed into it.

Yancey had to feel miserable but he was nice to me. He put his arm around me, shook my hand and congratulated me. The most pleasing thing about winning that day was when Palmer finished the 18th and came over to me. He gave me a little hug and said, "Congratulations. You won the big one."

Then he finished his card out. As he walked off he hitched up his pants and the people fell out of the stands.

There were thousands around the green and five police-men escorted me through the crowd to the clubhouse. I hadn't had so much attention from the cops since I backfired my 1949 Ford on North Central Expressway when I was fifteen.

I had about twenty minutes to try and calm down in the USGA office before we went out for presentations. At the ceremony I sat next to Nicklaus and I can't remember what we talked about. I had seen him before but I had never talked to him.

The U.S. Open victory meant a big silver trophy, $30,000 prize money and the opportunity to win it again someday and prove my week at Oak Hill wasn't just a fluke. It also meant the mass-interview treatment in the press tent. I was still nervous and I was a completely different person, not smiling and answering questions straight on. Later I loosened up and we had some fun.

Someone asked how I would spend the prize money.

"I may buy the Alamo," I said, "and give it back to Mexico."

Hey, people remembered that back in Texas. When I went to San Antonio for the PGA championship a few weeks later everyone kept mentioning the Alamo, so I took a tour of it. When I came outside, I said, "Well, I'm not gonna buy this place. It doesn't have indoor plumbing."

I got away with that one better than I did my wisecrack a few years later when I went back to Rochester to be inducted into the Oak Hill Hall of Fame. They plant an oak tree in your honor and put your name on a plaque in front of it. So there was my tree out there with Walter Hagen's and Ben Hogan's.

"Thanks very much," I said, "but it probably will be my luck that this is the only tree the dogs use."

I never dreamed that tournament would do so much for my career. It gave me a tremendous amount of confidence.

One, because it was the first one I ever won, and two, because of the caliber of the golf course, tournament and players. And since it was the U.S. Open, it gave me the impression that other tournaments wouldn't be as hard to win. Still, I never dreamed I would win twenty-five more tour championships in the next thirteen years.

When we were finished with all the celebrating in Rochester, I called Bill Eschenbrenner in El Paso and told him I wanted to come home soon and play golf with all my friends. I thanked Bill and Herb Wimberley for helping me get my Class A card, and he told me he'd get everybody together whenever I could get there.

A few weeks before, when I had been at Horizon Hills, I noticed Martin Lettunich was having trouble with his swing. I tried to help him. "Lee," he said, "I don't know any Mexican who can play golf."

I walked off, took a thirty-gallon barrel of balls to the other end of the range and started hitting them at him. Martin thought it was funny.

Well, when I went back there as U.S. Open champion, Martin asked me on that same practice tee, "Lee, what am I doing wrong?"

"Martin," I said, "I don't know any Mexican who can play golf."

8.
Super Mex,
Super Mess

The first time someone mentioned endorsements to me on the tour I didn't know what he meant. After I won the U.S. Open I learned real quick.

That championship opened the door to big money and fast living. It was a real kick for a while, but I'm glad that a few years later I decided to cut back on the fast living before I ran out of the big money.

No one ever wanted to manage me until I won the U.S. Open. Suddenly I looked real good to guys eager to make some deals for me. Very quickly—maybe too quickly—I decided to go with Bucky Woy, a really bright guy from Akron, who was one of the greatest negotiators I've ever seen. He'd work around the clock on something and he'd never get discouraged. You could throw him out the door and before you knew it he'd come in a window.

Bucky had some good ideas, like nicknaming me Super Mex. At Cleveland, a couple of weeks after the U.S. Open, I walked to the 9th hole and saw kids in the gallery waving signs: SOCK IT TO 'EM, SUPER MEX! It stuck, just like my pal John Homorsky nicknaming my gallery Lee's Fleas.

Bucky also had some bad ideas, like convincing me to withdraw from the Canadian Open the week after the U.S. Open. I was playing so well I probably could have won, but Bucky persuaded me that if I played badly in Canada and missed the cut, people would say I was a flash in the pan. To make it worse, I actually went to the Canadian Open, played a practice round and then got out of the tournament by telling a pack of lies. I told the officials that my daughter was sick and I wanted to go home.

What I did in Canada in June of 1968 is one of the two black marks I have against me in all my years on the tour. The other was my refusal to play in the Masters, which I'll get to later. In the case of the Canadian Open I've been able to go back to the tournament and create great rapport with the people. I've won that championship three times and today I'm probably the Canadian Open's biggest supporter.

By the time I went to Cleveland the next week, I had signed a letter of intent with Bucky, a commitment saying he would be my manager. He would receive 15 percent of any money I made from deals he negotiated for me but none of my golf winnings. Bucky got right to work, which meant I didn't enjoy the Cleveland tournament. He wouldn't let me leave my motel room. He didn't want anybody talking to me because he was busy negotiating contracts.

Meanwhile, I was getting all sorts of attention from the press and the public. I liked that at first, but they began to take more and more of my time and it became very difficult for me to go to the course and follow my regular practice routine. I couldn't hit balls and putt for a couple of hours without being interrupted every few minutes by an interviewer or fans asking questions and wanting autographs. I know everyone was curious about me, but it took me a while to learn this was something I'd have to live with.

I've been interviewed in some of the funniest places in the

world. I've even been in the bathroom, sitting on the commode, and there would be a guy outside the door, asking me questions. But over the long haul the media has been great to me.

As soon as I made it big, I wanted a logo. Arnold Palmer had the umbrella, Jack Nicklaus the golden bear, and the late Tony Lema had the champagne glass. I picked the sombrero and had it copyrighted in the U.S., Canada, Great Britain, Japan, Mexico, Australia and most other Free World nations. That was a good idea because today my sombrero logo appears on products I endorse all over the world.

But when I first cashed in on my name I had four major contracts—with Faultless golf equipment, Blue Bell clothing, Dr Pepper and Dodge cars and trucks. This was the start of a lot of big-money years and everything seemed great then. I had a lot to learn.

Faultless signed me first, paying $50,000 for one year to endorse a new line of equipment carrying my name. But they spent so much time gearing up for production, advertising and promotion that my contract was over just when they were ready to market everything. They came back and said, "We'd like to extend your contract three years at the same price." I said, "No, that dog's not going to hunt in this field." I wound up with $100,000 a year for the next three years.

My Faultless deal has lasted longer than any other but it's a funny thing. The company has had three different ownerships and my latest contract runs through 1984, but I have never been involved in designing their golf clubs. They have one of the best club-makers of modern times in Toney Penna and they've chosen to use me in other ways.

I spent eight years with Blue Bell, but I made little from that deal because I didn't receive any front money or an annual fee. Rodger LaMatty, the president of the corporation, was a good friend and I went into it strictly for a percentage of the sales. The sports clothing business is very competitive, so I never made much.

Bucky set out immediately to land the best possible deal with a beverage company. He sent letters to Coca-Cola, Dr Pepper, Pepsi and Seven-Up pointing out that I had played golf with a Dr Pepper bottle and that I could be a good representative for their product. Coca-Cola came after me first, simply because they are very intelligent in seeking athletes they figure are going to be in the limelight for a while. But they only offered me something like $10,000 a year for three years. I believe they were going to put me on the shelf and wait to see if I became a superstar.

Then Dr Pepper became very interested. Naturally, they liked all the publicity I had given them—but the fact that I had Dallas roots and Dr Pepper is a Dallas-based company also influenced them. It would have been a slap in the face for them if Coca-Cola, Pepsi or Seven-Up hired me, and they offered a very nice deal: $50,000 a year for four years.

I had a great relationship with Dr Pepper. I did a lot of clinics and TV work for them, including some grocery store ads. I usually filmed those at one o'clock in the morning when the store was closed and cleaned. Two or three people were hired to push shopping carts around while I did my dialogue. It was a lot of fun. Once, when they had a distributors' meeting in Dallas, I gave an exhibition on the front lawn of their headquarters on Mockingbird Lane, hitting golf balls with that old 32-ounce family-size bottle.

But I had to quit demonstrating that on a regular basis because they quit making the bottles with very thick glass. I could still take a bottle with thinner glass and hit the balls, but I taped the neck of the bottle and wore a glove on my right hand to protect me from broken glass. The trouble was that kids emulating me would pick up a bottle, throw the ball up and crash! The bottle would break and cut their hands. We agreed it was time to stop.

I really messed up the first television commercial I filmed for the company. They were shooting it on a practice green at Upper Montclair, New Jersey, and it was to be a one-minute spot. Just before they turned on the cameras they put a bunch of cue cards in front of me. That was the first time I had seen the script and I was nervous. My first line was, "Hi! I'm Lee Trevino!" but for the life of me I couldn't get that out. Finally, the producer cut that minute into segments and we did it, but I was never very comfortable with it.

The Dodge deal paid $40,000 a year and furnished my family with two cars. I got a lot smoother on those commercials. I began working with Don Schwab, a producer who never bothered with cards on the set. He said, "You're getting paid a lot of money for this. The least you can do is memorize this thing." Don has been a tremendous help to me through the years.

With all my Dodge commercials, I'd walk in and whsssht! I'd do 'em clean. I not only learned my lines but everyone else's, too.

Later, Bayer Aspirin paid me $50,000 to do two commercials in one year. I did one at the pool table in my house in El Paso. I said, "Hi, I know how to miss a two-foot putt, but I didn't know what to do for a headache until I read this medical journal about Bayer Aspirin." Every time I missed a short putt after that somebody would holler, "Hey, Lee, you need a Bayer!"

I went to New York for the other one and they wanted it in Spanish. I looked at those words on the teleprompter and said, "Wait a minute! What the hell is this?"

The guy said, "That's your commercial." And I told him, "I don't read Spanish. I'm very lucky to speak it."

Luckily, they had a Cuban script girl. She worked with me for ten minutes and I knocked it right out. They sold a lot of aspirin with that thing in Florida, Texas and California. But I would have had a big headache myself if she hadn't been there.

I might have won a second major championship that summer of 1968 if I hadn't been so caught up in all the excitement at the PGA tournament in San Antonio. I was anxious to play in my home state, and San Antonio, with its large Mexican-American population, gave me a hero's welcome.

The city fathers met me at the airport and a mariachi band was playing when I got off the plane. They bused about 1,500 kids out there and they were screaming and yelling. That was in the morning. After sundown the tempo really picked up.

Arnold Salinas, Bucky Woy and I were staying in rooms right beside the golf course at Pecan Valley and a lot of the guys in the Pan American Golf Association came down from Dallas. We had parties every night and everything was pretty crazy. At a press conference someone asked me if I brought my wife. "Naw," I said. "You don't bring a ham sandwich to a banquet!"

Next morning the long distance operator woke me up. "Hey," Clyde said, "this is ham sandwich." Man, it took me a while to smooth that over. Our marriage was shaky and my mouth made it worse.

My head just wasn't working real good that week. Despite all the drinking and hell-raising, I shot some good rounds and was just a couple of shots out of the lead starting the last round. But after what I pulled the night before I was lucky I even found the first tee.

Gatorade was new on the market, and the local distributor brought us three cases. Some of the guys were mixing it with everything just to see how it tasted.

I drank beer most of the night, however, and then went to bed. A lot of beer can make you thirsty and I woke up at four in the morning, cotton-mouthed. I opened the refrigerator to find something to drink and saw a saucepan full of Gatorade. Man, I thought that was perfect. I lifted that pan by its handle and damn near emptied it. What I didn't know was it was mixed with tequila. I was drunk as a skunk before I could get back in bed.

The temperature was more than a hundred degrees when I teed off with Arnold Palmer that afternoon and I just tried to stay out of his way. He had a good chance to win, too, and he wasn't drunk. Arnold had never won a PGA championship. It was the only major he'd missed, and he wanted it badly. But he hit a bad shot to the left on 18 and Julius Boros beat him out of his chance to win. Me, I shot 76 and fell back in the pack. Arnold and I left Pecan Valley feeling terrible, but for different reasons.

Life was moving fast in those days. Too fast.

A few weeks later I was living it up at another party. This time Clyde was with me and we were sitting at a piano bar in Harrison, New York, with my pal Ted Makalena. I had drunk a lot, but Ted, a teetotaler, was just there for a good time. He and Clyde were singing "Tiny Bubbles," the Don Ho song. We stayed until one or two in the morning. Ted, who had failed to qualify at Westchester, told us before we left he was flying home to Hawaii the next day. We agreed to meet again in Las Vegas in a couple of weeks.

Later that week Bill Eschenbrenner called me from El Paso.

"Lee, I wanted to let you know about Ted's accident," he said. "He drowned at Waikiki Beach."

I was stunned. He had just been with us, as full of life as always.

He died in a freak accident. Ted was one of those thick Hawaiians, maybe a little taller than me, who was strong and perfectly conditioned. He had a hairline fracture in the upper part of his neck from a high school football injury but it hadn't bothered him in years. He was standing in waist-deep water, about fifteen or twenty feet from shore, and he had two of his kids standing on his shoulders, waiting for a wave so they could dive in. It seemed one kid dived a little sooner than the other and snapped his neck.

Ted blacked out and fell face down in the water while his kids swam to shore. No one else was paying much attention because at that beach you see a lot of people lie down in the water in a prone position and let the waves bring them in.

But after Ted stayed out there a few minutes they went after him. They rushed him to a hospital, but the oxygen to the brain had been cut off too long.

It was such a tragedy—a fine young man with a wife and three kids wiped out in a matter of minutes. I had to figure it simply was his time to go. The Lord wanted him and there is nothing more you can say.

I've joked about how I survived being struck by lightning. "I'm a reject," I said. "The Lord didn't want me." But I believe it works like that. It was time for Ted, but not for me.

When Bill Eschenbrenner told me about Ted, I said, "I'm going to win the Hawaiian Open and give Ted's kids some money to go to college." Bill probably thought to himself, "Yeah, Lee. Sure you are." But when we got to Honolulu in November I was determined to do it.

I was interviewed before the tournament and I said, "I think it will take 16 under par to win, and I plan to shoot it."

That's exactly what I did. My 272 earned me $25,000 and I donated $10,000 for his son when he graduated from high school. That meant a lot to me. When Ted died, it was like losing a brother.

That night I felt lonely thinking about old friends. I picked up the phone and called Hardy Greenwood in Dallas. We hadn't talked to each other in more than three years, since our argument over his refusal to sign my application for a Class A card.

His wife, Gray, answered and I said, "Hi, how are you?" She never forgot my voice. "Lee!" she said. That really sounded good. Then Hardy got on the phone and we talked like nothing had ever happened. He's that way and I'm that way. We had a good visit and I told him I'd come by the driving range to see him the next time I came to Dallas.

When I left Honolulu the next day, I felt better.

My problem with the Masters is a perfect example of my talking too much and then psyching myself out. Augusta

Lee Trevino

Virginia Hunt

The house where I lived as a boy
in Dallas.

As a Little League baseball
star, 1951.

Clint Grant, *Dallas Morning News*

Building pitch 'n' putt course in 1955:
Hardy Greenwood (left), me, Norman Scott.

As a U.S. Marine recruit
at age seventeen.

TENISON MEMOR

MUNICIPAL GOLF

Lee Trevino

With U.S. Marines 3rd Division golf teammates, 1959:
Bill Irwin with cup; in rear, from left, Ed Percival,
me, Bill Spencer.

Joseph A. Salinas

Reunion at Tenison Park: with
Dick Martin (left), Bill Gray (right).

United Press International P

On the way to my first major victory, I sink a birdie to capture the lead at the 1968 U.S. Open.

United Press International Photo

I entertain the gallery during the
1971 U.S. Open with my "discovery" of a snake
in the grass. I carried the toy snake in my
golf bag and dropped it in the rough.

At Muirfield, Scotland, in 1972, during
the British Open, I register disbelief at a
missed putt. But I would go on to win
my second Open title in a row.

Jack Nicklaus congratulates me on my
playoff victory in the 1971 U.S. Open. I shot
68 to win by three strokes.

Trevinos at home. From left: Claudia, me, Troy, Lesley, Tony.

Sam Blair

With four of my Salinas "brothers," from left: Joe, Arthur, Arnold, Albert.

With Andrew and Angie Salinas.

With Hardy Greenwood.

Joseph A. Salinas

Charlie Buchanan, Copyright © Golf Digest/Tenn

I wince after a shot went wrong in the 1974 PGA
championship, but a lot of others went right. When it was over
I had won another major championship.

National is a lovely course in the U.S., second only to Green-Brier in beauty. The course is in magnificent condition, the tournament has a wonderful tradition and the gallery is the most knowledgeable in this country. But each April when I drive up Magnolia Lane toward that old white clubhouse I feel the Masters closing in on me again. And all because I acted stupidly in 1969.

If I never win the Masters, it will be my fault. If I'd had a different outlook, I think I could have already won there. It may be the most prestigious tournament, but it has the weakest field of any tournament we play in this country. With all those old Masters champions and foreign players invited every year, there aren't as many strong contenders. Yet the fact remains that I have played very few good rounds at Augusta National.

My Masters mess was typical of my general performance in 1969. After working and playing my ass off all those years to reach the top, I found myself on a pedestal. I was nervous as hell, feeling a lot of pressure to win and drinking too much Scotch. When I played poorly I never blamed my own mistakes.

I missed the cut in the U.S. Open at the Champions course in Houston, the one my buddy Orville Moody won. I was defending champion and there I was, packing up and leaving on Friday. But that didn't compare with my problem back in Augusta.

Through the years a lot of people have thought I hate the Masters, the city, the people and everything in Augusta. That's not true. Actually, I really liked the Masters when I first was invited to play in 1968. And in 1969 I received some great news before starting the final round on Sunday, April 13: our son, Tony, had been born. I whooped and hollered, "I'm gonna win this tournament for him!" I did shoot a 69, but I was so far back I would have needed a 59 to win.

A few days later I was in the locker room at the Tournament of Champions, talking to Charlie Sifford. He was complaining about the invitation policy of the Masters, which at that time never had had a black player qualify for a spot in its field. Charlie was the top black player of that period and he was upset that the former Masters champions, who together can invite one player each year, had never chosen him. Then I started talking about the course.

I said I didn't like it, that I didn't think I'd ever have a chance of winning there, and that I didn't think I'd ever play there again. I thought I was just letting off steam in the locker room. What I didn't know was that Bob Green, the Associated Press golf writer, was nearby and heard what I said. The next day my comments about the Masters were carried on the wire all over the world.

At first I was really angry with Bob Green because I thought I was having a private conversation. In the years since, we've become good friends but at that time it really upset me that everyone knew what I had said.

Clifford Roberts, the tournament chairman, said he was sorry I felt that way but that I would receive an invitation to play in the Masters as long as I was eligible. Then I made it worse by refusing the invitation in 1970 and 1971.

I should have just swallowed my pride and gone on and played. But I felt everyone was wondering if I was as good as my word, so I had to stick by my guns. That was the greatest mistake I've made in my career.

The first year I stayed away I played in a local PGA event that weekend in Las Cruces, New Mexico. I won $200 and had some fun and people may have thought, "Hey, ol' Lee is really sticking it to the Masters." But I was only hurting myself.

I changed my mind in March of 1971 but because I had refused the invitation in January I missed the tournament again. Jack Nicklaus had a lot of influence on me. We were playing a charity exhibition match at The Breakers in West Palm Beach, Florida, and he sat me down in the locker room for a talk. I've always worshipped that man. I've idolized

Palmer, too, but Nicklaus has been a closer friend. When he talked, I listened.

"You just don't know how good a player you are," he told me. "You can win anywhere."

I thought about that and it turned me around. I started playing the Masters again, but I still had a defensive attitude for a while.

During my first practice round the next year a police captain stopped my caddie, Neal Harvey, and tried to kick him out. Neal was wearing one of the ten tournament tickets I had bought but the officer said that was the wrong ticket for a practice round. I told the captain, "No, you ain't kicking him out. If he goes, I go."

The captain and I argued in the middle of the eighth fairway and, man, my chili was hot. Well, he left to talk to some officials, who sent some practice round tickets out for Neal.

Since Clifford Roberts ran the Masters with an iron fist, I found him and asked why a tournament ticket didn't cover practice rounds. He said they always sold out of tournament tickets in advance and they felt they should keep practice round tickets separate and sell them daily. I told him I'd be happy to buy them but no tickets were sold at the main gate where players drove into the club. He said, "Well, we just don't do it that way at the Masters."

I told him, "Hell, I don't need this. I'll leave." I walked off and got in my car and had Neal put all my stuff in it. People were all around my car now. The press had picked it up and asked me about it. I was still mad and saying things I shouldn't have said. If someone had come to me five minutes later and offered me a chance to give $5,000 to charity and take back all my words, I would have accepted gladly. But it was done and the story was out: TREVINO RAGING AT MASTERS AGAIN!

Well, I stayed and played the tournament but it was pretty damn tense. People were watching my every move, listening to every word, wondering if I would explode. When I didn't go into the clubhouse, they thought I was boycotting the place.

That wasn't the reason at all. I always take a room near the Augusta club, so I wait until forty or fifty minutes before I tee off to go. Since I have to park right next to the driving range, it's more convenient to put my spikes on when I leave my room. Then when I get out of my car I'm right on the practice tee. What's the sense of getting out of your car there, walking all the way to the locker room to put on a pair of shoes and then walking all the way back to where you started?

I was rude to Clifford Roberts a few times when he wanted to talk. Once he sent someone to the practice tee with an invitation. "Mr. Roberts is having coffee in the clubhouse and he'd like you to join him," the man said. Without even looking up, I said, "Just tell Mr. Roberts I don't drink coffee." That was stupid, but I did it.

One afternoon he met me as I came off the course and asked if I would like to see Bobby Jones' trophy room. I really didn't, but I sensed he was trying to show that everything wasn't as bad as I had made it out to be. I just took a deep breath and went with him. We spent about fifteen minutes together and that was the extent of it. In the later years before he died I saw him once. I was hitting some bunker shots and he came over, shook hands and said, "Nice to have you."

I have played in the Masters peacefully for quite a while now, but I still don't like the course for three reasons: it has no rough, the hills favor the long hitter, and the course favors a player who hooks the ball.

If they had rough at Augusta National I believe I could have won there. But there's no rough to bother anyone who hits some stray shots. Bobby Jones didn't want rough. He felt if you missed the green and had the right touch you could get the ball up and down. Now I don't believe in rough around the green, but if a man misses the green or the fairway by thirty feet, he damn sure should be penalized by having to hit his ball out of rough.

The short hitter is at a disadvantage because he has to hit it into a bank off every tee. The long hitter flies his ball over the hills or puts it on top of them, while a short hitter flies his ball into them. The long hitter is looking at a level or downhill lie and the short hitter an uphill lie, a more difficult shot.

Gary Player won the Masters and he doesn't hit the driver any longer than I do. But he can hook his irons, which you must be able to do because the greens slope from left to right. You need to move the ball from right to left. I worked two weeks on hooking my irons before one Masters and actually led after two rounds, but my luck didn't last. I'm at my best hitting a fade.

People have said, "Jimmy Demaret won at Augusta with a fade." And I said, "Jimmy Demaret didn't have to beat all those long hitters I have to beat today." Those guys beat me on the par-5s.

Look at how much Nicklaus and Tom Watson have won there. Now Fuzzy Zoeller and Seve Ballesteros should win the tournament quite a few times because they hit it long and don't have rough to contend with.

So Augusta is one type of golf course and I'm another type of golfer. Even on our best days, I guess you'd say we have our differences.

It's strange how even in my off years I always managed to win a tour event. In 1969, I still won at Tucson and finished seventh on the money list with $112,418. And in 1970, when I still wasn't sure how good I was, I finished first in money with $157,037 and won the Vardon Trophy for the lowest scoring average on the tour, a title I took three more times in the next four years. And I won two tournaments—Tucson again and the National Airlines tournament in Miami. Now there was one hell of an adventure.

I was one shot out of the lead after the third round and that Saturday night I went to the jai alai games with some British golf writers. We left at two o'clock, then went back to the hotel and stayed up drinking until five in the morning.

That afternoon I shot a 68 and tied Bob Menne. Then I beat him on the second hole of the playoff when I made a par and he made a bogey. My caddie, Neal Harvey, rushed over and shook my hand. "Man," he said, "that is the greatest athletic performance I have ever seen." I was so tired I wanted to walk on my knees but my day was just beginning.

I had to be in El Paso the next morning to give a deposition because I was parting company with my manager, Bucky Woy. The only way I could make it was to catch a five-ten flight from Miami to connect with a late-night plane out of Dallas.

A police car was waiting for me. In fifteen seconds I grabbed the trophy, said thanks and goodbye and jumped into the car. That cop was a fantastic driver. He weaved through heavy traffic at a hundred miles an hour with his siren screaming. I got on the plane just as they were closing the door.

The stewardess smiled at me. "Busy day?" she asked. "Yeah," I said, "kinda busy."

I was in court in El Paso the next morning, giving that deposition. Bucky was a sharp manager and a really hard worker but he tried to get too big too fast. Don Whittington wasn't happy just to be the manager of the home office and let Bucky negotiate those contracts and collect 15 percent. He wanted to handle the job himself and let our company operate without Bucky. I was influenced by that, but we still had to reach a settlement with Bucky, who was due money for the life of all the contracts he had negotiated. It was another difficult situation, typical of how my life was going.

We agreed that I would pay him $168,000 over an eighteen-month period and we would tear up his contract as manager. It was a tax write-off for me, and Bucky seemed happy with it. We're still good friends. I'll always remember he thought of the nickname, Super Mex.

When I arrived at Merion in June of 1971 I was thinking about what Nicklaus told me in March: "You just don't know how good a player you are. You can win anywhere." I also remembered what Walter Hagen once said: "Any player can win a U.S. Open, but it takes a helluva player to win two."

I had thought about that a thousand times since I won at Oak Hill three years before. Merion is a great old course on the Main Line in the Philadelphia suburbs, and as soon as I played a practice round there I felt this might be the time for me to move up in class.

I thought I had an excellent chance of winning because my game was starting to peak. At some point in the year your game will always peak, and mine had started to do it the past few weeks. Until then I had been in a semislump that started back in 1970.

That may seem a crazy thing to say about a year when I led the money list and won the Vardon Trophy, but a lot of my success came early in 1970. I won both my tournament championships during the first three months of the tour and then fell back. That's why I didn't qualify for the Tournament of Champions in April of 1971. There the field is made up of winners dating back to the previous Tournament of Champions. That week I said, "What the hell, I may as well go to Tallahassee and play."

Those people down in Florida put on a fine golf tournament for the guys who don't qualify for the Tournament of Champions. My game was sharp at Tallahassee and so was my attitude.

The night before the pro-am a young magazine writer came by my motel room to interview me for an instruction article. "I don't think you'll ever see me in a tournament for losers again," I told him. "It's time I started winning. I can feel it coming."

I won at Tallahassee and started rolling. I played well in Houston, Dallas and Fort Worth and then I won again at Memphis. When I reached Merion I had my putting stroke back, and my confidence. Merion suited me best of all the courses I had played at that time. It was relatively short—just over 6,500 yards—but with extremely high rough and small, well-contoured greens it demanded accuracy. And, like at Oak Hill, I got a break when it rained during the week. That softened the greens so that I could stop my low ball, which I always hit. With my flat swing I've never been able to hit the ball high.

A great example of how those soft greens helped was the 9-iron shot I hit on the 12th hole in the fourth round. The ball landed 20 feet past the flag, but I put backspin on it so it sucked back and stopped about four inches from the hole. With the kind of play around the greens, it came down to accuracy off the tee in order to win the tournament. If I kept my ball in the fairway, I had a fine chance.

I played extremely well that Sunday. I started the round in third place, two shots back, and I played in a twosome just ahead of Nicklaus and Jim Simons, the young amateur and college star. Simons was leading when we teed off but began to falter. It came down to Jack and me to decide the championship.

I played a little better than Jack, but he kept making some par-saving putts behind me to stay close. I had a one-shot lead through 17, and I felt if I could par 18 I would win because that was a helluva tough one for anyone to birdie. Merion's 18th probably was the most difficult finishing hole in U.S. Open history—a 458-yard par-4. You had to carry a small brook with your tee shot and the fairway started about 180 yards out. There was a double-tiered green with the lower tier in back, a very deep bunker on the right and a couple of bunkers on the left. And out-of-bounds was only about 15 feet left of the green. If you hit your ball over there, it might wind up on the veranda of the clubhouse.

I had just made a difficult downhill putt to par 17 and I hurried to the 18th tee, anxious to get on with it. I teed up my ball, stepped behind it and threw some grass up to see which way the wind was blowing, never taking my eyes off the driving area. That gave me a mental picture of how I wanted the ball to go. Then, with my eyes still fixed ahead, I put my hand out for my driver. This was a habit with me. I expected my caddie to put the grip right in my hand, where I could grab it, put it down and hit my ball.

Well, nothing hit my hand. I put my hand out again and nothing hit it. So I took my eyes off the fairway and looked around for my caddie. He wasn't there.

Just then, he squeezed through the crowd with my bag. He was a young law student who hadn't done much caddying and the pressure was getting to him. He had stopped for a drink of water.

"My God, where have you been?" I said.

Once I finally hit the ball I cut it just a little too much. It was a low fade down the left side of the fairway and my ball stopped half in the semi-rough, half in the fairway. As I studied my shot I heard a huge roar from the gallery back at 17. Nicklaus had made a helluva putt for a par, and to a lot of people it looked like he was going to steal the tournament.

If the ball had been sitting up clean, I probably would have hit a 2-iron or 1-iron and tried to roll it to the green because there was an opening between the bunkers in the front. But I decided to hit a 3-wood, cut it low and try to run the ball through the opening to the flag, which was in the back of the green. It was too much club and the ball hit near the gallery in back and bounced. There were so many people they couldn't move and my ball went into the crowd. I had a pretty good lie because all the grass was stepped down and my ball was sitting up. I chipped it up short and was left with a 6-foot putt. It was the type I dislike the most, one breaking from left to right, but if I made it I had a par and Nicklaus would be under tremendous pressure to birdie the hole and tie me.

I walked around it, stalked it and got ready to hit the ball. There must have been 20,000 people around the green but they were so quiet you could hear a pin drop. There was a sign that said, "No Cameras, Please" nailed on a tree behind the green. A young man had climbed up and was sitting on it about six feet off the ground. Just as I got ready to hit the putt the damn nail came loose and he fell. It distracted me and I pulled away from the putt.

"Is he all right?" I asked. Somebody said, "Yes. No problem." But my concentration was broken. I didn't hit a good putt and missed it to the right.

I holed out for a bogey, giving me par-70 for the round and 280 for the tournament. Now Nicklaus could beat me with a birdie. He already had hit his drive long down the middle of the fairway, and it looked like he could hit a 5- or 6-iron into the green. The pin placement wasn't that difficult. It was in the dead middle, and if he pitched his ball in front, it was going to run down to the hole because of the slope.

I signed my card and ran into the locker room. Nicklaus had left his iron shot 14 feet short of the pin, and if he sank the putt, he had won another U.S. Open championship. I couldn't stand to stay out there and watch him.

It was a very warm day and the locker room wasn't air-conditioned, so all the windows were open. I heard the crowd go silent and I stood there with my eyes closed. Then I heard thousands of voices go up: "Ah-h-h-h . . ." And then down: "Oh-h-h-h!" I opened my eyes and grinned. "Now we've got a playoff," I said. I began thinking about another 18 holes on Monday. This is the only U.S. tournament that has not changed to sudden-death.

I saw the putt on film and to this day I don't know how

it stayed out. He hit a great putt down that slope but it hung on the left side of the cup and slid two inches past.

In the press conference afterward, we were kidding back and forth and someone asked me, "What do you think your chances are in the playoff?"

"My chances are just as good as Jack's," I said. "The pressure is on him. He's the best ever, the odds-on favorite. If I lose, people expect it. If he loses, it makes me look like a hero."

What the hell, I thought, I might as well try a little reverse psychology.

When we waited at the first tee the next day, I felt it was my time to win. He had scrambled a lot in the fourth round to tie me. But I was nervous. We had five minutes until tee time and my glove was soaked from sweat.

I was joking with the crowd while I reached in my bag for a fresh glove. I found a rubber snake in there that I bought my daughter at the Fort Worth Zoo a few weeks earlier. I had pulled it out on the 18th green at Colonial and scared Miller Barber's caddie, Herman Mitchell, so bad that he damn near ran into Crampton's Lake.

I slipped on the fresh glove and then held up the snake. Everybody laughed, including Nicklaus. "Throw that over here and let me see it," he told me. I tossed the snake to him, he looked it over, shook his head and threw it back to me. The next day a lot of stories said I scared him with that snake.

The way I played the first hole you'd have thought *I* was scared. I pushed my 9-iron into the bunker and then missed my putt, causing me to settle for a bogey. Jack drove the middle of the fairway, left his second shot 15 to 20 feet from the hole and two-putted for a par.

But on the next two holes he hooked his ball into the left bunkers and hit some poor shots, trying to get out. I parred both holes and took a one-shot lead. But, more important, I realized he was nervous, too.

But when I bogeyed 6 he pulled even. Then on 8 I left my second shot six inches from the hole and birdied to take the lead again. I was in control the rest of the way. I made a 35-foot putt on 12, a 25-footer on 15 and then I rolled a 65-footer just inches short on 16 to save a par. I believe Jack could see he had run out of holes. He bogeyed 17 and I took a 3-shot lead. This time I had no trouble on 18. I hit an iron into the front bunker but I blasted the ball out and it landed just four feet from the cup. It was the easiest putt in the world.

I finished with a 68, still three shots ahead of Jack, and I had my second U.S. Open championship. Hello, Walter Hagen!

Jack was very gracious when he congratulated me. "You played absolutely fantastic," he said. And the crowd loved it, even though it was mostly the wealthy, country-club set. The American dream is to see the underdog win, but you find that happening less in a sport like golf. And I believe my victory pleased the average fan across the country. I represent the public golf courses, the working man, the blue-collar worker.

That playoff taught me something else. The good Lord doesn't give you everything. He kept one thing from Jack Nicklaus: his sand wedge. He's a poor wedge player, out of the fairway and out of the bunker. If he had been a good wedge player, I sure wouldn't have beaten him that day at Merion. He left his ball in two bunkers and chili-dipped two wedges.

But the Lord kept a hook from me. I might even have won the Masters if I had that.

I had to fly to Cleveland that night, so my only celebration was drinking a few Scotches on the plane. But the next day during a practice round I enjoyed one of the special moments of my life.

Bob Goalby and I never had been close. When I first came

on the tour he didn't appreciate my loud, outgoing ways. When I won the U.S. Open in 1968 he wasn't impressed. "In five years," he told someone, "we'll be playing benefits for that guy." But now he was running across two fairways to see me.

"I want to shake your hand," he said, "and I want to tell you one thing. That was the greatest exhibition of golf I've ever seen. I'm proud of you."

The next week I was entered in the Canadian Open at Richelieu, just outside Montreal, and I really wasn't interested in playing. I was anxious to get on to England and start practicing for the British Open.

The first day at the Canadian I couldn't get myself started. I just chopped it around and shot 73. I wanted to withdraw, but remembering what I had done to the Canadian Open in 1968, I said, "Aw, I can't do it again." I figured I would stick around one more day, miss the cut, then go on to the British Open and no one would say anything.

Well, a funny thing happened. I shot 63 in the morning and the wind changed 180 degrees in the afternoon. A lot of scores went up and all of a sudden I found myself in contention. "I may have a chance to win this thing," I told Clyde. Then she showed me all the clothes she had bought shopping in Montreal and I knew I needed that $30,000 first prize.

On Sunday I was two shots behind Art Wall when I teed off. I caught him down the stretch, but I missed an 8-foot putt on 18 to give him a chance to win. He needed to sink a 7-footer. But the crowd was moving so much that he pulled his putter away and waited. "Fore, please!" I yelled, trying to calm them down. "This tournament's not over yet!" He leaned over the putt again. He missed it. We went back to 15 to start a sudden-death playoff.

I birdied the hole with a 20-foot putt, coming down the side of a hill, and I'll be damned if I hadn't won the Canadian Open, too.

Clyde and I hurried back to our hotel, the Queen Elizabeth, to change clothes and then hustle to Toronto to catch a nine-thirty flight to London. But there was a formal cocktail party in a suite down the hall and René Longpré, the hotel's director of sales, wanted us to come in for a drink.

"René," I said, "I'm not dressed for a party like that and we have to catch a plane."

"Don't worry about it," he told me. "We'll get you packed and have a limousine ready to take you to Toronto."

So I walked into that party with my shirttail out, my hair a mess and no shoes on, and started holding court with all these people in fancy gowns and tuxedos. If I had been some guy off the street they would have thrown me out the window.

We had some drinks and then raced for our plane. That night, as we flew across the Atlantic, we were drinking beer and relaxing. "Well," Clyde said, "what do you think?"

"I'm going to wind up winning all three of these things," I said. "I just won the U.S. Open and the Canadian Open on courses I'd never seen. Now we're going to Royal Birkdale and I know that course. There's no way they're going to beat me there."

I had good reason to like Birkdale. I had played there twice in 1969, in the Alcan tournament and Ryder Cup matches. It was a seaside course with some sand dunes, and you had to hit your driver very straight there. If you kept the ball low, letting those sand dunes shelter it, the wind wouldn't affect your shots. It had five par-5s, and I could reach all of them, which was something unusual for me.

I couldn't wait to get there. Hell, it was Tenison Park without trees.

9.
The British
and Me

Everything went like a dream that week at Royal Birkdale, but that really was no surprise. My experiences with British golf through the years have captured a special place in my heart.

I was introduced to British courses in 1968 and it was love at first sight. My strong showing in championship tournaments just made the romance more glamorous. And after I had played in a dozen British Opens I saw no end to it.

"I'll always play in this tournament," I said before I teed off in 1981 at Royal St. George's. "I don't care if I shoot eighty-eighty. I'll always play over here. I love this championship. I love the links courses, with the mist and wind sweeping off the sea. I love these people."

There's nothing quite like playing in the British Isles. Golf is in the air there. You breathe it, like smelling home cooking. It makes you hungry. You want to play.

Now it seems strange that I passed up my first spot in a British Open. I earned that in 1968 when I won the U.S.

Open, but I had a commitment to the Milwaukee tournament and didn't think I should break it. I did go to England for a couple of tournaments that fall, then entered my first British Open in 1969 at Royal Lytham and St. Anne's. In 1970 we played St. Andrews and I led after three rounds, but blew the championship with a final 77. Still, I felt I eventually would win the British Open. Once I got a taste of those seaside courses I knew they were for me.

It doesn't matter if you hit it short. As long as you hit it straight you can run the ball on the greens. And the wind doesn't bother me because I hit a low ball anyway.

As fond as I am of Birkdale, Muirfield, where I won the 1972 championship and finished second to Tom Watson in 1980, is my all-time favorite. I play the courses in Scotland extremely well. I can bump and run the ball better on them than any native. I've told the people there, "If you believe in reincarnation, I probably was a Scotsman two hundred and fifty years ago."

I won British championships the last two years they used the small ball. That was one more thing I loved about playing there. The ball was 1.62 inches in diameter as compared to 1.68 for the American ball and that meant less wind resistance, fewer dimples on the ball and less spin. To me, playing with the small ball was like cheating.

While I was always comfortable on the courses, I had some early problems communicating with the people. It took me a while to loosen them up, too. They were pretty damn reserved when I first went over there.

During my first practice round for the Alcan tournament at Birkdale in 1969, my caddie told me, "You have to be careful here because there's a birn going across the fairway."

"A what?" I said.

"A birn," he said.

I hit a drive, then walked down the fairway and found my ball in the water. I looked at him and said, "Why didn't you tell me there was a creek running through here?"

"I told you, mate. That's a birn."

The 9th is a blind hole. You go over a hill and down and you can't see the fairway. I stood on the tee for a second, then asked him, "Where is the fairway going?"

"Hit it straight to the marquee," he told me.

"Where?" I asked.

"Hit it to the marquee," he said.

Well, I took my driver and hit my ball into the right rough. "Damn," I said, "I thought the fairway went this way."

"No," he said, "I told you that a straight line off that tee is to the marquee."

"Let me ask you a question," I said. "What the hell is a marquee?"

"That thing over there," he said, and he pointed at a tent.

I knew right then I had to learn the language.

He wasn't a very good caddie, though, so I got rid of him after nine holes. That's when Willie Aitchison took my bag.

Willie was a Scot who had carried for two British Open winners, first Tony Lema and then Roberto de Vicenzo. Since Roberto wasn't playing in this tournament, I hired Willie and he wound up working for me in Britain and Europe for many years. But first I had to teach Willie how to caddie.

"I've got too many shots and I hit the ball too many different ways," I told him. "Look, I want you to go to the drugstore . . ."

"Where?" Willie asked.

"Go to the drugstore," I said.

"You mean the chemist's," he said.

"Well, just go there and get a notebook," I said. "Bring it out here tomorrow and I'll show you how to diagram each hole and mark down the yardage."

Willie handled that all right, but there was one problem. He talked more than I do.

"Willie," I said, "you've got to be the listener. We can sing together, but we can't talk together."

He still got involved with talking to too many people. In the Ryder Cup matches at Birkdale in 1969, Miller Barber and I played Tony Jacklin and Peter Townsend and when we came to 18 it was almost dark and we were feeling a lot of pressure. These points were important because the teams were tied and the United States hadn't lost to Great Britain since 1957. When I got to the tee I looked for my bag and Willie wasn't there.

The next thing I knew here comes a guy carrying my bag and I've never seen him before. "Where's Willie?" I asked.

"He was talking to someone coming up the hill," this stranger said, "and he slipped down and broke his ankle." Now that's got to be a first in the history of golf!

While I was still trying to figure that out, I missed an 8-foot putt to keep us from winning outright and that let Great Britain tie us, 16–16. Hell, the British should have given Willie a team blazer.

When I went to London to play in the Piccadilly Invitation in 1968 I didn't know much about the tournament except that it was very exclusive. To play there you have to have won one of the four major titles in the past year, be top money-winner for the previous year or something like that.

Before I got there I played in the Alcan, and the Piccadilly publicity man looked me up. I was wearing slacks, cowboy boots, sports coat and sports shirt with no tie, which is what I liked to wear. He wrinkled his nose.

"My good man," he said, "you'll be staying at the Savoy Hotel during the Piccadilly and this is not proper attire."

I asked him what he meant by that. "You must wear a solid suit," he said. I told him I didn't have a solid suit, didn't even have a tie. He gave me a fishy look and walked away.

Well, before I checked into the Savoy, I went to Moss Brothers in London and rented me white tie and tails, top hat, cape and cane—the whole bit. Then I made a big entrance at the hotel and got a whole lot of press.

The publicity man was kind of stunned, but he introduced

me to his wife. She told me I must go sightseeing and kept telling me about the Teems. I didn't know what she was talking about.

She pointed out a window of the hotel and said, "That's the Teems."

I thought she was pointing at a building, but she told me she was talking about the river that goes through London. I told her, "Lady, that's a little ol' creek in Texas." She didn't even know what a creek was.

My British Open victory in 1971 really warmed up the fans, and I think I've had a lot to do with galleries' behavior since then. They've gotten louder, more sociable.

Oh, they were sociable before, but only at the right time and the right place. Galleries were completely different from those in America simply because they have been brought up to believe golf is a very quiet game. You don't talk while anybody is playing, and you sure don't laugh.

Families would come out to watch golf and they might not speak to each other for hours. At my first British Open I was struck immediately by the quietness of the galleries. They were huge, but silent. They were all bundled up in raincoats and boots and they all looked like brothers and sisters. There might be 30,000 people out there, but you never heard a word.

Through the years, because of my strong play in tournaments and the television exposure I've enjoyed with my own show on the BBC, I have gotten the galleries to enjoy themselves more. They have tremendous knowledge of the game. In Scotland once, I hit a beautiful low shot that carried about three or four feet above the ground, right at the flag 190 yards away. The ball hit in the front and just trickled over the green and stopped about four feet off the green but 20 feet from the hole. I got a standing ovation. The guy I was playing with hit a terrible-looking shot that hit the bank and kicked down about four feet from the hole. Nobody made a sound. They knew it wasn't a good shot.

In the United States you'll probably find only 30 percent of the galleries really care about the game. The other 70 percent are just where it's happening, man. It's like a flea market. Look at the Colonial tournament in Fort Worth. It's one of the best in our country, but half the people who go to it never see a golf ball hit. Especially those girls parading around in shorts and halter-tops. They don't give a damn about golf.

When British youngsters come to you for an autograph they never hand you a gum wrapper or a paper bag or a napkin. Every one of those kids has an autograph book. Some of those books go back a hundred years and have been handed down through the generations. I don't mind signing those. They make me a little piece of their family history.

The British and I are on pretty familiar terms now, but occasionally I still shake someone up.

I have a good friend in England named Jack Aisher. He's chairman of the board of Marley's, which is a British chain of tool-and-supply stores, and he likes to throw a dinner party when we're filming my show for the BBC. One year we were at Gleneagles and Clyde and I were having a swell time. Everyone was making toasts, something the British dearly love to do.

"To the Queen!"

"To the Prince of Wales!"

Well, I listened to that for a few minutes, then I grabbed a glass, stood up and shouted, "To Paul Revere!"

Some huge, fat guy with a walrus mustache started coughing and sputtering, "My man! My man!" I leaned over the table, patted his shoulder and said, "Aw, I'm just kidding you!"

Jack Aisher, who knew me better than his guests did, laughed like hell.

At Turnberry in 1977 we stayed in a hotel on a hill with a gorgeous par-3 course below. Clyde and I would play it in the afternoon, then climb about a hundred and fifty steps to the hotel. When we reached the top, people would be gathered there, watching us.

"Well," I said, "no sex tonight! Any man who walks a hundred and fifty steps doesn't have strength to do anything."

And I've always been fascinated by how the British dress up for golf tournaments. Even the greenskeepers.

All the years I worked on a golf course I always wore the raggediest clothes I could find—old blue jeans, T-shirts, boots. But the guys mowing the fairways and greens there are wearing coats and ties. It's customary. That's why I go to Britain with a coat and tie on and I leave with a coat and tie on.

On a plane I never know if I'll sit next to some chairman of the board who may be looking for someone to endorse his company. If I'm dressed in blue jeans and a T-shirt and he asks me what I do for a living, he'll look at me and forget it. I'm the last person he wants to endorse anything.

It's none of my business what other athletes wear, but I couldn't believe how John McEnroe was dressed when he flew back to New York from winning Wimbledon. He looked like he'd been working on his car.

Someday these guys are going to realize you don't make nearly as much money in the sport as you can make outside. That's why I carry a three-piece suit and three sports coats with matching ties. A lot of times I have to go to two or three functions in a week and I don't have to wear the same thing. My wardrobe has changed some since I went to that U.S. Open in 1967 and could wash everything for a quarter.

Tradition never changes at the British Open, however. Those people have a tremendous respect for history, rank and honor.

When we played at St. George's, I was walking toward the Tented Village, where equipment and clothing companies sell their products, to make an appearance at the John Letters exhibit when I saw an ancient little man totter by wearing a dark blue uniform. Hell, he had a big gold sword buckled around his waist and six or eight rows of huge, fancy medals on his chest.

I thought to myself, "He better hope there's no lightning around here."

But if lightning ever did get him, I guess he certainly would want to go in full dress uniform.

Everything is so old there. St. Andrews, of course, is the birthplace of golf. It is home of the R&A—the Royal and Ancient Golf Club of St. Andrews, which has held the Open since 1860. At Muirfield the Honourable Company of Edinburgh Golfers wrote the Thirteen Articles, the first rules of golf, about thirty years before some of our guys wrote the Declaration of Independence. And St. George's, on the English Channel, is only a couple of tee shots from Pegwell Bay, where Julius Caesar first landed in England. There also are a couple of castles in the neighborhood where Henry VIII hung out.

My locker in that old clubhouse was so small that all I kept in it was a pair of shoes, which I stood on end, and a bottle of whiskey for Seve Ballesteros' father.

"Man," I told the attendant, "I can't get my one-iron in this locker!"

But when it's time to play the Open, I don't want to be anywhere else.

The R&A still held the Open championship from Wednesday through Saturday in 1971 and my last day and night there were an unforgettable ending to a wonderful week.

Clyde and I stayed at the Prince of Wales Hotel in Southport that week. Just across the road was the Kingsway Casino, which was owned by George James, a man who treated us wonderfully. We went there every night to have dinner, see a show and then gamble until five in the morning. Then we went back to our room and slept until noon. I'd eat a light lunch and leave for the course around two. I teed off about three-thirty every day so everything worked out. I had some fun, I got some rest and I was always ready to play golf.

Jimmy Dean, the singer and actor from Texas, came over from London, where he had a role in the Sean Connery movie *Diamonds Are Forever,* and we spent a lot of time with him. Then, out of nowhere, Arnold Salinas appeared in the locker room at Birkdale just before I teed off in the second round.

Pete Dominguez, a good friend and a great guy who owns some Mexican restaurants in Dallas and Houston, had made so many bets on me with everyone at the Great Southwest Club that he sent Arnold over to coach me. He bought him a first-class airline ticket and said, "Go keep Lee company."

Pete's an extremely generous guy. One night in Dallas we were drinking pretty good and I was admiring his '49 Ford pickup. "It's yours," he told me. "That thing's a collector's item!" I said. I protested and tried to give it back the next day but he wouldn't hear of it. I still drive it and it's in top condition. I do all the work on it myself.

I don't know how Arnold talked his way into the clubhouse because security was extremely tight. But he can get in anywhere. All I know was I was sitting on a bench putting some cleats on my shoe when I heard a voice behind me ask, "Hey, are there any Mexicans in this tournament?"

I turned around and there was Arnold. "All right, son!" he said. "Go get 'em!"

I shot 70 that day, same as Tony Jacklin, and we were tied at 139. I finished strong the next day and my 69 put me one shot up on my old friend from Formosa, Mr. Lu, and Jacklin, who was wavering a little. Nicklaus was back some more with 71–71–72.

The weather was beautiful for the final round, just like it was all week. It must have been the best in British Open history: sixty-five or seventy degrees every day. I came out to the first tee in shirt sleeves and Mr. Lu, who still had a crewcut, was wearing a straw hat.

We first met in 1959 when I was a Marine stationed on Okinawa and we played a match on Taiwan. Mr. Lu beat me, 10 and 8. He was a fine golfer, a great up-and-down player, and a wonderful little man. Those British galleries loved him. He called me Bird, a name he gave me when I was in the Marines because my drives always flew past his.

We shook hands on the first tee and I told him, "You don't need this trophy. You'd just fill it with flied lice." He grinned. "Birrrddd!" he said.

I shot 70 and beat Mr. Lu by one shot with a total 278, but the final numbers were deceiving. I had a 5-shot lead with nine holes to play, but I was clowning so much I almost threw it away. It was just one of those times when everything was fun and I figured it was going to work out okay. And it did.

I was so hot on the front nine that I was hitting putts and walking away to the next tee without watching my ball drop in the cup. "Hey, Bird," Mr. Lu said. "You want to go through?" I laughed and hit him on the back of the head.

Just before we made the turn I knocked in a long putt and it snaked into the hole. I tossed my putter up, fell to my knees and then face down on the green. That's when the gallery loosened up. They loved it! No one had ever done that on one of their greens.

Well, it was so much fun by then that I almost forgot to finish the tournament. Clyde and Arnold walked along the fairway with me the last three rounds, thanks to the courtesy of an R&A official, so they were right there. On the back nine I would three-putt a hole and think, "Hell, I've got enough to win." Then on 17, I hit into a sand dune, knocked it across into the rough, had a hard time getting out of the heather, then stopped a 15-foot uphill putt short and wound up with a double-bogey 7. Suddenly, my lead was down to one!

The last hole at Birkdale is a par-5 of 500-plus yards but

my chili was hot and I hit a drive that left me about 200 yards from the pin. Then I smoked a 6-iron to the back edge of the green. Meanwhile, Mr. Lu got unlucky. His drive kicked left into a bunker, and when he tried to come out, he hit his ball with the heel of the club and it exploded into the gallery behind him, hitting a woman right between the eyes. She went down like she was shot, bleeding badly. He was sick about it, and I couldn't even bear to look at her. It turned out she was all right but it was terribly unnerving.

His ball bounced back in front of the green, however, and he hit a sensational shot that stopped about six feet from the hole. I had a 40-foot putt but I didn't fear a thing. I knocked it to two and a half feet and I still didn't have any doubts that after Mr. Lu sank a birdie putt he forced me to make mine to win. I didn't wait. I just knocked it in and walked away. Clyde and Arnold ran up and hugged me.

"Hey, we did it!" I told Arnold.

"I know you did," he said.

I won my first British Open championship with a game as good as Jack Nicklaus told me it could be. So in just twenty days I had beaten Jack in our U.S. Open playoff, taken the Canadian Open title and then won in Britain, where Jack was defending champion.

"I wish," he told a huge crowd at presentations, "I had kept my damn mouth shut."

We had a marvelous party at the Kingsway Casino that night. Someone had given us a two-gallon bottle of Bollinger's champagne at the course, so we drank that and then ordered some more. I had some special guests coming—two nuns from the local orphanage.

George James had told me, "If you win this tournament and give five hundred pounds or fifteen hundred dollars to the orphanage you will really make a hit with them." Well, my prize money was $13,000 and I told the nuns I would give them $5,000 of it on one condition: they had to come to the casino and drink a glass of champagne with me.

They had never been in a bar in their lives but they did it and had fun. Everybody was raising hell. Mr. Lu was there and Jimmy Dean was singing to me. Later that night we raffled off my golf clubs for $1,500. I gave that to the orphanage, too. I wanted to share my joy.

Nicklaus tied for fifth at 283, but he was really fired up when we went to Muirfield for the 1972 British Open. I believe Jack felt if he ever was going to score a Grand Slam of the four major championships he would do it that year because he would play on his favorite courses—Augusta National, Pebble Beach, Muirfield and Oakland Hills, where the PGA was held later that summer.

I had given him a tough battle for the U.S. Open title at Pebble Beach for three rounds but I weakened the last day, which wasn't surprising. I had spent four days in an El Paso hospital with pneumonia before the tournament and got out of bed just in time to fly to California and practice for nine holes. But in the month before I defended my British championship, I trained very hard. I took my family with me to Central Texas, rented a house and trained on Orville Moody's place in Killeen. I was up at five every morning, running through the hills, and then I played golf. The greens superintendent had a twelve-year-old daughter, a mute who read lips, and she drove the cart with my bag on it. I didn't ride. I ran between shots and I played 36 holes a day. I was determined to be sharp for Muirfield.

Well, I won again at Muirfield with 278 and again I broke out of a 36-hole tie with Tony Jacklin after shooting 71–70. It turned around in the third round. Jacklin had a good edge on the front nine but I sank a 25-footer for a birdie on 14 and that touched me off. I birdied the last five holes and finished with 66 to lead Jacklin by one.

On 16 that day I gave a pretty good example of getting a lemon and making lemonade. I took a 6-iron and just as I got ready to hit my shot the grip unravelled at the bottom. Like a snake, it just tangled up around my hand. It was a funny sight and everyone laughed. I stopped, took a couple of minutes to rewrap it and got my muscles tensed up. When I swung that club it felt like a feather and I hit a bad shot into the bunker, on the back upslope. I had no shot from there so I went with my wedge, hoping to keep it on the green, maybe 30 feet from the flag, and 2-putt for a bogey. I hit the wedge and the ball came out entirely too fast but somehow it hit on the green, took one big hop and went into the cup on the fly. It went in so fast the BBC cameraman missed it.

Coming out of there with a birdie instead of a bogey meant two shots that changed the final outcome because the next day Jack rallied with a 66. But my 71 gave me the championship by one.

That ruined possibly the best shot at a Grand Slam in his career but Jack didn't take that loss as hard as he did losing by one to Tom Watson at Turnberry in 1977. I finished fourth that year, after sharing the 36-hole lead with them, but I was pleased with that because I was working myself back to top form after my back surgery. For me, that was a good tuneup for the Canadian Open, which I won. For Jack, it must have been very tough to play head-to-head with Watson the last 36 holes, shoot 65–66 and see Tom beat him with two 65s. What marvelous golf they played! The whole locker room was out there in the gallery watching them play.

That trip had its special value for me, just as every one to Britain does.

In 1981, for example, I tied for twelfth at St. George's and won $10,000, which just about covered expenses for making the trip, but I made deals to play in other tournaments around the world paying a total of $150,000 appearance money.

And there's the pleasure of meeting nice strangers and making new friends I'll always remember.

My golf series on the BBC has gotten me into a lot of

homes. I have old women and old men walk up to me on the course every day and say, "I've never met you and I know nothing about golf but I love your television show. I had to come out and meet you."

The most gratifying part of my week at St. George's was meeting the Millenstead family—Keith, Margaret, Tracy and Sean. They have a home in Sandwich Bay, right by the course, and Arnold Salinas and I spent the week there. Sitting in their home, talking and having dinner every night, really made the trip. Jack Aisher and Keith are good friends and Keith, who owns a garage in Sandwich, takes care of Jack's cars. Keith is a left-handed golfer, about a 9-handicapper, and he told us a funny story about trying to join Royal St. George's Golf Club.

It costs very little to join—about $500—but first you have to go through certain procedures. You have to have eight members endorse your application. Then it goes before the board. Then you have to play a round of golf with the captain of the club. Well, the captain looked at Keith's application and noticed his occupation was garage owner.

"I'd like to have a word with you," he told Keith and they went into his office.

"There's no sense in going any further with your application," he said. Naturally, Keith wanted to know why.

"Well, my good man," the captain said, "it's your occupation. You're a tradesman."

They didn't allow working stiffs in the club. They wouldn't dream of having a member who runs a filling station.

The funny thing was that I got Keith tickets for the clubhouse because he was driving me to the course every day in his Mercedes. One day he was in there having a beer, sitting at a beautiful glass table. He set his glass on a coaster on the table and was really enjoying himself when a steward came over to him.

"Sir," he said, "we don't do that here at St. George's."

Keith wasn't wearing a coat and tie like everyone else. He

just had on a shirt and sweater. "Oh," he told the steward, "I'm sorry. I'm not a member and I didn't know."

"I can see that, sir," the steward said.

"Well," Keith told him, "when I'm at home having a beer I use a coaster and put it on my glass table." And the steward, very softly, said, "Exactly, sir. Exactly."

Keith laughed about it. "He just buried me right there," he said.

There's so much I like to remember from all those visits. When I played in the 1973 Open at Troon we stayed on a farm where they were harvesting hay. I had no place to practice, so I would go down in the fields and hit balls. The Scot who farmed the place had two sons, about fourteen and eight, and they wanted to play golf, so I got them some cut-down clubs.

The old man looked at them, puffed on his pipe a minute and said, "I thank you, Mr. Trevino, but I don't know when these lads will have a chance to use them. There's w-o-r-r-r-k to be done."

Those kids worked, all right. The older boy drove the tractor and stored the hay in the barn. The little one fed the cattle and milked the cows. As soon as they got home from school they took off their uniforms, put on their coveralls and worked until dark. And they were up at five in the morning, picking strawberries.

They'll never be kids, just like me. Looking back on my early years, I believe that's why I have such a special relationship with kids and with other people. I'm forty-two years old and I still act like a kid, because I never was one.

There's a kid in me trying to get out. Maybe there always will be.

10.
Lost and Found

Johnny Carson hasn't forgotten the first time I was on his show, but I wish I could. Better yet, I wish my wife would.

He introduced me and I came out from behind that curtain walking like John Wayne. Sideways. I went over to shake hands but that little stage where Carson and his guests sit was too much. I tripped on the first step and almost landed right in front of his desk. Carson threw up his arms like the set was caving in.

"Oh, my God!" he moaned.

I was stumbling, falling down drunk on national television. Elaine Stritch, the actress, was on the show with me and she didn't give one of her all-time great performances either. She got off on me pretty good, saying she liked little Mexican guys because they made wonderful elevator operators. To show her she couldn't outwit me, I propositioned her before millions of people.

We were talking back and forth and Carson couldn't get

in a word. Finally, he just stood up and said, "Would you two just shut up?"

How could this happen? It was the night before the Westchester tournament and I was some kind of hero. This was the summer of 1972 and I had just won the British Open again. The next day I was paired with Ben Hogan and everyone was excited about that. It seemed the perfect time to be on the Carson show.

Jesse Whittenton was at Westchester with me and Monty Strange, my driver and valet, and we got to New York early that evening. We stopped in a bar across the street from NBC and I drank four or five fast Scotches. Then we went over to get ready for the show.

We were in the Green Room, the hospitality room for Carson's guests, and everyone was drinking like sailors. I asked for Scotch but they didn't have any, and somehow I wound up drinking cognac. I'd never drunk cognac in my life.

Elaine Stritch had her maid with her and two little poodles on a leash, and was having a great time until they told her she was going on the show in five minutes. She told the girl to bring her dress, then stood up and dropped everything she was wearing except her underclothes. The girl held up her new dress, she got in it and hurried off.

When I got out there I couldn't even see the audience. I don't remember what I said but it must have been bad. Clyde was sitting at home in El Paso, watching the show, and to this day I think she believes I took that girl out. Oh, she's never forgiven me for that!

I remember driving back to the hotel in New Canaan, Connecticut, after the show, feeling tired and depressed. It was one of those times when you realize life at the top isn't as rosy as most people think. Maybe I was on the verge of a nervous breakdown. I was very busy and people were pulling at me from every direction. I did twenty-three commercials that year and had a heavy schedule of tournaments, cocktail parties, dinners and television interviews. The only satisfaction I was finding at the time was drinking Scotch. I couldn't find time to relax enough before I had something else to do.

Sitting in the hotel bar late that night, I told myself, "Why are you doing this? You need some time off. Why don't you just jump in the car and start driving south?"

So I left my clothes in the room and Monty in bed and took off, leaving the Westchester tournament behind. I remember being on the New Jersey Turnpike until I got so sleepy I couldn't go any more. I saw a motel sign, pulled in and went to bed.

I woke up at three in the afternoon and I didn't know where I was. The only thing I could do was call my wife.

"Well," Clyde said, "where are you?"

"I have no idea," I told her.

"Look on the phone and give me your area code and phone number," she said. I did and she told me, "I'll call you right back."

First, she called the motel manager and got the location of the place and made sure I was all right. Then she called me again.

"Leave the car there and take a cab to the Newark airport," she said. "There's a ticket waiting for you at the American Airlines counter. Just stay on that plane and I'll join you in Dallas. We're going to Acapulco."

We spent a week there, playing golf, swimming and just sitting around and relaxing. When I got back I was ready to play again.

That was the closest I have come to crashing and burning, but it wasn't the end to my heavy drinking. For years it was a way of life for me.

Once at Atlanta I was on the 16th tee, it was raining and already seven o'clock. We'd had two delays that day and it didn't look like we'd finish the round. I went in the locker room, wet to the skin, and asked for a Scotch and soda. Before I knew it, I'd had five.

Then it was eight-fifteen, and suddenly they said, "Get back on the course. You're going to finish."

I said, "Get back where? You gotta be joking. I'm drunk!" But I went back out there, parred 16 and birdied 17 and 18. And I couldn't see the ball!

I loved to drink any time, any place. At my first British Open, Bucky Woy had an adjoining room and he put a big bottle of champagne outside his window to chill. I crawled out on the ledge and stole his champagne and brought it back to my room. Monty Strange and I drank it, then I filled the bottle with water and wrote a note: "Thanks very much. It was fantastic." Then I crawled back out on the ledge and put the bottle and note outside Bucky's window—six stories up.

There were times when I finished tournaments with horrible hangovers. I won the National Airlines championship once on the first playoff hole after staying up until five that morning. I lost the PGA at San Antonio in 1968 when I had drunk so much tequila I could barely see the tee. But in 1974 I realized I was living too fast and that this was going to cut years off my career. I quit hitting the hard liquor all the time and became more selective with my beer drinking.

Oh, sometimes during a tournament I forget and down quite a few. After the third round at the 1981 Tournament of Champions I stayed in the locker room with John Mahaffey and John Brodie, the television commentator, for hours, then went to my room and found that Joe Salinas had ordered me a pizza and a banana split. So I turned on the TV, ate the cold pizza, drank the banana split, which looked like a rainbow with all the ice cream and syrup running together. Then I fell asleep. The next day I felt fine and I won the tournament.

I have a constant weight problem and I know shorter players usually don't last as long as a flat-belly like Don January, who's six one and is still competitive past fifty. It's tough for a shorter player to do well after forty. Look at Gary Player. He's a perfect physical specimen but he's only five six and a half and four years older than me. I saw the problem coming some years ago and changed my drinking habits.

Now if I want a lot of booze I'll go to Mexico, sit under a coconut tree and stay drunk for a week. Most of the time on the tour I just like to drink some beers after the tournament on Sunday.

But nobody can make a career of shooting out the lights every night and winning on the golf course the next day. Sure, I've heard about how Walter Hagen partied all night and then played great golf. But I don't believe it.

There's no way Walter Hagen could have liked it more than I did, but I learned there was a limit. Old-timers will say, "I know he did it. I was there." But Hagen couldn't have done half those things and played championship golf. That's like Doug Sanders and his reputation. If Doug had done just 25 percent of what he got credit for he would have been dead at the age of thirty-two. And Hagen could not have played a game of nerves and lived it up the way people said he did every night.

Walter Hagen probably was a helluva psych artist. They said he came out to play a match in the morning, carrying a fifth of whiskey and still wearing a tux. But I'll bet that he went to bed at ten o'clock the night before, got up at six to put the tux on, then went outside and fell in three bushes to get it dirty. Instead of putting on shaving lotion he probably splashed himself with Jim Beam and carried the bottle to the first tee. Remember, all the big tournaments in his day were match play and half of match play is psyching the other guy out.

Don't get me wrong about Doug Sanders. That man has had some fun. He had the flashiest clothes and the flashiest women. Every lady friend I ever saw him with could have been Miss Universe. He always was a big spender. When he was playing the tour he kept apartments in five or six cities.

I spent the night in his place in Dallas once. All he had in it was booze and about a hundred and fifty pairs of golf shoes.

But his drinking and partying weren't as wild as his reputation. Sure, he carried a briefcase filled with miniature bottles of Scotch, bourbon, gin and vodka. He called it his Medicine Chest. But that was as much for his friends as for himself.

His career as a world class golfer ended with the British Open in 1970, when he was thirty-seven. He missed a 3-foot putt on the last hole that would have won the championship, and the next day he lost the playoff to Jack Nicklaus. Fast living may have shortened his career a little but his short backswing was the real cause. He's the only player I've ever seen who hit a ball lower than I do. He had great legs, wrists and forearms but he began to lose strength in his legs as he got older. And he had wrist surgery and had to take cortisone shots. There was more to it than wild living.

Then there's someone like Lon Hinkle, who might not have done a thing if he hadn't changed his way of life. A few years ago we were playing in Mexico and Lon pulled one of the funniest things I've ever seen at a golf tournament. But it also was one of the dumbest. He had finished about fifteenth and won $300, and at presentations in the clubhouse they called his name. Lon had drunk a lot of beer by then and he had a tough time walking to the front of the room to accept his check. He hit five or six tables and knocked over some chairs but he finally got up there. The president of the Mexican PGA presented the check and Lon, who's a big guy with a baby face, stood there smiling like he got caught with his hand in the cookie jar.

"Ah," he said, "three hundred dollars!" He held the check up, tore it into about forty pieces and threw it into the air like confetti at a parade. Then he stumbled back to his table.

In those days Lon Hinkle was still so poor he couldn't pay attention. He not only threw away the money but was rude.

He and I really weren't close friends then but I grabbed

him the next day and said, "Lon, you're going to play a lot of golf over the years and you can't act that way in front of people."

"What did I do?" he asked me. He couldn't remember a thing.

We started playing practice rounds together on Tuesday on the tour and we were paired in some of the tournaments. I could see the talent this young man had but he wasn't making the cut. Then I found his big problem. He couldn't wait to get home to San Diego. There's a bar where all the sports people hang out and he loved that place. I told him, "You've got to get away from San Diego. If you eat hot dogs, you're going to play like a hot dog. You've got too much talent to waste it like this. You've got to move to Dallas. We can practice together and I can teach you different shots, when to take a risk and when to do this and that."

Lon liked the idea. Pretty soon he was settled in Dallas with his new wife, Edith, a girl he met in Switzerland. His career began to take off. In 1979, he won the Crosby and the World Series of Golf, and his tour earnings came close to $250,000, almost three times what he won in his first six years combined. Before the 1981 PGA championship he won the National Long Driving competition with 338 yards, six inches, and collected $10,000. So he has found he can make money and still have a good time. We've become very close too. He's just like family.

Maybe the PGA championship I won in 1974 balanced the books for the one I threw away in 1968 when I gulped down all that Gatorade spiked with tequila in my midnight thirst and then staggered out and played a lousy final round. Lord knows I certainly approached the week differently.

We played it at Tanglewood, in Winston-Salem, North Carolina, and I liked the course. Tanglewood is a lot like Merion. There are two or three long holes and that's it. But what I liked about it was the rough. It was a foot high and uniform, probably the fairest rough I had seen in America.

And I liked my living conditions, even if they were quiet. Better yet, my landlady, Mrs. Mayberry, loaned me a putter that helped me win the tournament. I rented her house for myself, Albert Salinas and the Ely family, some very special friends from Charlotte. There are five of them—Jim and Sue and their three sons. They fixed my meals and we relaxed together in the evenings. My mind was on golf, but one thing bothered me. I couldn't even make a 2-foot putt.

I had been looking for a Palmer-Wilson putter with the original grip on it, a kind that was only made in 1959 or 1960. I opened the door to a storage room in that house and saw a golf bag on the floor with a putter sticking out. Damned if it wasn't the Palmer-Wilson with the original grip that I wanted. I asked Mrs. Mayberry if I could use that putter in the tournament and she said fine. But she wouldn't sell it to me because it had belonged to her late husband. I used it in a practice round and made everything. In the first round I shot 73, but the next day I began to warm up with it. I came back with 66.

"Do you think I could buy that putter now?" I asked Mrs. Mayberry that night. "I putt awfully well with it."

She smiled. "If you win the tournament," she said, "I'll give it to you."

I shot 68–69 for 276, beating Nicklaus by one after some heavy rain. I still have that famous Mayberry putter.

The tournament had an odd finish. I rarely hit a hook well but I hit a terrific one on 17, the only dogleg left on the course, and I've never seen Jack more surprised. My ball went down the middle of the fairway and I had a 4-iron to the green. I 3-putted from 20 feet, however, because the soft greens were full of footprints, so that cut my lead to that one shot.

He hit first on 18 and used a 3-wood, which I couldn't understand because that would make him hit a 2-iron to the green. Then I saw his psychology. He wanted to put pressure on me by putting his ball in the fairway. I just put my ball on the peg, took my driver and hit it about 290 yards up the middle of the fairway. Jack missed with his 2-iron off to the right and my 6-iron stopped about 25 feet behind the hole. Then, for the only time in my career, I putted out to win the championship without giving Jack and Hubert Green, the third player, a chance to putt out.

I had a simple reason. I was choking so badly that the putter was actually jumping in my hand. When I hit that long putt 18 inches past the hole there was no way I was going to mark the ball and look at that putt for another five minutes.

I stood right in the middle of the green and looked at Jack and Hubert and told them, "I'm coughing and leaking oil so bad that if I don't putt this thing out now I'm going to faint."

"Go ahead and putt it," Jack said. So I did, and it was over. That was my fifth major championship and I won it without a fifth of Scotch.

Clyde is never going to be a weak wife who shudders when her husband yells. She's strong and she can make decisions, as she did when I was so mixed up after that Johnny Carson show. She can take care of herself, and I like that. We've had our ups and downs and we've had some knockdown drag-outs but now we have a strong marriage. It's a marriage that probably is going to last until we die.

She's a battler. I learned that years ago. When I got to drinking that Scotch at parties I always thought I was invisible. I had a bad habit of talking to girls and flirting with them even though Clyde was there. Girls would come up to me, wanting my autograph, and I would sweet-talk them. *Hi, sweetheart. My, you look good. What are you doing? I'd like to have your number.* And blah-blah-blah. She never confronted me with it or said anything. But the first time I saw her talking to a guy, I exploded like Mount St. Helens.

It was two in the morning and we'd been drinking for

hours at the Knights' Club in the Rodeway Inn in El Paso. Clyde and I were there with Don Whittington and his wife, Claudia, and we were ready to leave. Don and I went out, but when our wives didn't follow us I went back to see what had happened.

Well, I saw Clyde and Claudia Whittington talking to two guys at another table and I went berserk. "Get outside!" I screamed. "We're going home."

It turned out they were talking to Claudia Whittington's cousin. Now Clyde was really steaming and we got into an argument driving down the expressway. She hit me across the face a couple of times with her fingernails and I was bleeding. She was driving and clawing me at the same time. I was mad as hell.

"Stop the car!" I said. "I'll get out right here."

"Good!" she said and slammed on the brakes. She stopped right in the middle of the expressway and I jumped out. Lucky I wasn't on Central Expressway in Dallas. I'd be dead right now.

A Holiday Inn was on the other side, so I jumped the median and walked over to get a room. While I was checking in I wiped my face with my coat, trying to get the blood off. All the people there recognized me and I felt like a damn fool. I stayed there a couple of days before I went back home.

Another time, in Pensacola, we got into it one night over a drink and she left me with some scars across my cheeks and nose that had all the pros in the tournament kidding me. "Ooh, you must have really got hold of a wild one last night!"

I did, but not the way they thought.

That Scotch did it again. We were sitting there, listening to the singer in the motel lounge, and it was almost closing time. The waitress came to our table for last call. My head already was bobbing like a cork on a fishing line so I didn't order anything. Clyde, who was feeling no pain, ordered B&B. When she got her drink and I didn't have one, I tried to grab hers. I don't even drink B&B but in my condition you could have put gasoline in front of me and I would have drunk it. But when I reached over for her drink, she grabbed it and put the glass between her legs. Then she looked at the singer again. So I reached over and hit the glass and spilled it in her lap.

She hauled off and hit me and I dragged her out of the bar. We were staying on the second floor and we got into a fist fight going up the outdoor stairs. It was like a Western movie. I pulled her to the top of the stairs and she was screaming. Lights were going on in all the rooms and people were looking out at us. Then they started pulling shades and locking doors.

When we got in our room we talked about it for an hour. I was totally out of line. The craziest thing I ever did, though, was to go to sleep. I'm lucky she didn't hit me with the chair.

Later we had a blast in El Paso after a New Year's Eve party at Jesse Whittenton's house. I thought I was invisible again, flirting with every broad in the joint. Clyde didn't say anything until Jesse was driving us home. I denied everything and that made her even madder. When I stepped out of the car she hit me with a right hook that buckled my knees.

But we smoothed all of this out some years back. We know now we can't fool each other. I believe we're as close as we are because there's no one dominant individual in our marriage. You show me someone who says, "We've been married twenty years and never had an argument," and I'll show you someone weak. You can't have a relationship like that. You've got to have disagreements.

The making-up is the best part of it. Once you've fought for two days you turn the lights down low and the music up high and lock all the doors and make sure the kids are asleep and then you have a little fun. That's what life is all about.

We've been married since 1964 and we've had a lot of arguments and, obviously, some pretty bad fights. But I think they bond the marriage and make us closer to one another. We respect each other to the point we can't bully each other.

And I've learned that Clyde has a great sense of humor.

A few years ago I decided to let a brokerage firm handle my investments and the first thing the company did was send me a long estate planning questionnaire asking in detail about what my wife and children would get if something happened to me. One of the questions was: "How would you describe your relationship with your wife?"

So I wrote, "Shaky—very shaky."

Then there was the question: "How would you want your estate divided if you should die?"

And I wrote, "That doesn't matter. If I die, I'm not going to leave my wife with all my money for her to run off to Europe with my best friend. I've got a contract out on her and a couple of her friends, so she'll be dead three days after I am."

The brokerage firm sent one of its guys to meet with me. Clyde was there, too, and she told him the same thing. "Lee's already told me he has a contract out on me three days after he's dead so I don't need any money."

I told the guy, "Look, I just want you to invest my money and tell me which businesses to invest in. I don't want you getting into my personal life. You can handle this without me telling you how many nights a week I sleep with my wife."

He said, "Well, I don't think there's any reason for this interview anymore."

Since Clyde is a good businesswoman she gets out a lot and stays involved in things. Once when I came home from playing in Houston I found some ribs thawing in the kitchen but no Clyde. It was one of those days when she had to meet with the architect and contractor on our new house and then go to our office and write the payroll. It was four in the afternoon and I decided to phone her and act mad.

She got on the line right away. "Hi," she said, "what are you doing?"

"Nothing," I said. "When are you going to be home?"

"Well, I'm still doing . . ."

"Let me tell you something," I said. "I've been gone and I'm tired. I want a home-cooked meal. I'm sitting here waiting on you. I haven't seen you in two weeks. You ought to be here with me. I don't like this one damn bit."

Next thing I knew I heard a buzz in my ear: m-m-m-m-m-m-m. She had hung up. Then she called right back.

"I think we had a real bad connection," she told me. "What was that you were telling me?"

That's how it is with us. We have great give-and-take and we have a lot of fun. We have three great kids and there's something new happening every day.

Our baby girl, Troy, was born in 1973 and I'll always remember her first communion when she was seven. It was the Saturday morning of the Nelson Classic and the whole family went with her to our church. It was a great sight: the priest in his robes and Troy going down front all in white, cleaner than the Board of Health.

Clyde had tears rolling down her cheeks. She leaned over to me and whispered, "This is so beautiful. Aren't you crying?"

"Why," I said, "do you think I'm wearing sunglasses?"

11.
Mister Wonderful and Friends

Caddies are a breed of their own. If you shoot 66, they say, *"Man, we shot sixty-six!"* But go out and shoot 77 and they say, *"Hell, he shot seventy-seven!"*

But I love 'em and I need 'em. A good caddie is very important to a professional golfer. It's like a legal secretary to a lawyer or a private nurse to a doctor.

I've always had a special feeling for caddies because I carried a few bags myself when I was a kid. I pay them top money, whether it's my number-one gun in America, a little black kid in South Africa or a lady in Japan dressed in white shirt and black necktie.

The caddie situation on the tour has improved a lot since I first went out there in 1967. Then a touring caddie might do a great job for a pro but he couldn't work in the summertime. It was customary to have local schoolboys or college students caddie at tournaments then. That was okay as long as the kids were qualified to carry a bag but the pros had a lot of complaints about their work. Too many of them made mistakes that took money from guys playing like mad to make a living.

For example, a player likes to mark his ball, then roll it to the front of the green. When the caddie gets there with the bag he picks up the ball and cleans it. Trouble was, a kid sometimes would pick up a ball that hadn't been marked. That was a 2-shot penalty for the player and those two shots could mean a lot at the end of the week.

Tournament sponsors realized it wasn't right to fire the regular caddies for three months and let inexperienced kids work, so they changed the policy. That was a relief for everyone. Too many guys drew caddies who only knew they had been told to carry that bag and follow that player. If a player walked down a fairway, the caddie would just follow him, and before you knew it he'd kick a ball or do something wrong.

Julius Boros may have had the funniest experience. He had a young kid who had never caddied before but was dead earnest about doing what he was told. Well, Boros hit a wedge on the first hole and took a divot out about eight inches long and three inches wide. He was walking by the divot and the caddie had the bag and was walking right with him because he had been told not to get three paces from his player. Boros looked down at the divot and said, "Pick that up." He assumed his caddie would replace it.

So they kept going and the kid carefully watched for divots after that. But about the 14th hole, Boros noticed his caddie was dragging his bag. He was gasping and bug-eyed. "What's wrong, son?" he asked.

"Mr. Boros," the kid said, "what do you want me to do with all these divots?"

But when you have the right man carrying your bag, you have a treasure. I've had three caddies in all my years on the U.S. tour, each good in his own way and each different: Ben Sessum, Neal Harvey and, standing five feet eleven and weighing in at three hundred pounds, my current man, Mister Wonderful, Herman Mitchell.

Herman is a couple of years older than me and an exceptionally good player. He's been caddying on the tour since 1957, starting with Gardner Dickinson. He was originally from Little Rock, Arkansas, and now spends some time in Memphis, where his brothers live, but he says his real home is that white line in the middle of the road. Herman was born to be a tour caddie.

Herman is smart. I'm talking streetwise, common sense. He's gruff but he's really gentle. I believe he has a complex because he's so heavy and people say things that upset him without realizing it. He and I have never had a cross word, but then, I understand him better than most people do.

Every morning I say, "Are you in a good mood today, Herman?" I tease him a little because he likes to chew on people. Someone else may walk by and say, "Herman, how are you?" and he'll say, "Why are you worried how I am?" Or, "Herman, how long you been caddying for Lee?" He'll say, "You writin' a book?"

When I went back to Baltusrol to play in another U.S. Open, I was walking up the 18th fairway on Saturday and the fans were giving me a nice ovation. Someone noticed Herman behind me and yelled, "Hey, Herman, you feel like carrying that bag another 18?" And he shouted back, "I wouldn't mind goin' two, three rounds with you!"

Herman eats too much, but Ben Sessum and Neal Harvey overdid in other ways.

Ben liked to drink, but he did a good job for me. I just made sure I always positioned him downwind. I hired him after I won the U.S. Open in 1968 and he was like me, young and enthusiastic. He's black but I called him a "passer." He was about as dark as I am. He wanted to go out and enjoy the lights, which was fine with me as long as he did his job. Ben worked for me a couple of years, then got married and settled down in Atlanta. That's when I picked up Neal.

Actually, I went back to my roots. I had known Neal since we were eight years old in Dallas. We were raised together, caddying at Glen Lakes. He was one of those kids from South Dallas who used to sleep over at my house on Saturday night. We were very close, like family, and we had some great times during the seven years he caddied for me. Neal made a tremendous amount of money, but he didn't know how to keep it. He was an adventurer, and a real high roller.

Back in the early 1970s I was paying him a regular salary of $200 a week plus a percentage of my purses. If I won a tournament, it was 10 percent. If first prize was $30,000 I would pay Neal $3,200 on Sunday night. Hell, on Tuesday he was broke and wanted to draw $50 on next week's salary.

Sometimes he got so involved in his social life that he messed up his job with me. When I won the Colonial National Invitation at Fort Worth in 1976, I gave him his money and told him to meet me in Memphis Monday afternoon. He drove and I always flew. He had put his car in the shop in Dallas for some work but he said he would pick it up in plenty of time to meet me in Memphis. Well, he was in his hometown with a pocketful of money and he was having a lot of fun. When I was ready to practice Monday afternoon, he wasn't there. I called the garage in Dallas and they said Neal had gotten the car at nine that morning, meaning he had enough time to reach Memphis by late afternoon. He finally showed up Tuesday afternoon after I'd played a practice round with Herman caddying for me. He told me the garage had kept his car so long that it made him late. I really got hot then and told him I knew better. Neal started crying. I told him to come on and let's start the tournament.

The next day I was off on everything. I played four holes and I kept going either over the green or short of it. I couldn't figure out what the hell was going on.

I said, "Neal, what kind of yardage do you have?" I knew I couldn't be that far off because I can tell how far I hit each ball, I don't care if it's an 8-iron, 6-iron, 5-iron or what. I can see the ball in flight. When a man tells me it's 167, I can come within three yards of hitting it 167.

Well, it turned out Neal was using the yardage card from Colonial Country Club in *Fort Worth*. I kept missing those greens and he kept saying, "Get it up and down for me, baby! Get it up and down for me!"

I told him, "Get it up and down, my ass! You'd better get your stuff together."

Neal was a good caddie and we won a lot of tournaments, but I guess it was time for a change. We had a lot of good times together and we were close. Maybe that was part of the problem. When you've been friends since you were kids, maybe you can't have a really good player-caddie relationship. I need someone out there to watch my moods, to pump me up or settle me down. Herman does that, but Neal wouldn't. He was a yes-man. He'd get mad along with me.

If I had a bad hole, I might say, "I hate this damn place anyway. I'm getting the hell outta here!" And Neal would say, "That's right. I don't like it either. Let's go!" He knew the faucet was running and I would give him $400 or $500 and he'd go party for the weekend.

Herman is just the opposite.

I've told him, "I'm blank. I can't play any more." And he would say, "Don't worry about it. Everybody has bad days. The chairman of the board has bad days. Multimillionaires have bad days. The Pope has bad days." Or I've made a double bogey and when we're walking to the next tee he would tell me, "That's history. Are you listenin' to me? That's history. Let's play this one." It lifts me right up.

We were playing L.A. one year and it looked like we were going to miss the cut. I had played in South Africa and Hawaii the past two weeks and I was tired and putting bad. I told Herman, "Let's go shoot 80 today and get the hell outta here!"

"Are you crazy?" he said. "Man, go out there and shoot 65. You can still win this tournament."

"Herman," I said, "I'm twelve shots behind."

"Golf is a funny game," he said. "People start backing up out there. You don't know what's liable to happen."

Sure enough, I made the cut, played real well the last two days and wound up making $7,500.

The problem with Herman is that he tends to second-guess a lot. When I hit a ball that doesn't come off right, I say to myself, "Goddammit! I hit the wrong club!" And he'll immediately say, "I knew it! I knew it wasn't the club!"

And I'll say, "Well, don't tell me now! Tell me before! The *world* knows it's not the right club now." Arnold, Albert and Joey Salinas all have told Herman, "Tell Lee if he's hitting the wrong club." And he says, "I ain't gonna do that. He's a great player."

My problem with caddies is I have too many shots. When I pull a club out I can make the ball go almost any distance I want. If it's 150 yards I can pull out a 5-iron but the caddie doesn't know if I'm going to punch it, hit a slow fade or what. If it's 180 yards and I pull out a 6-iron, the caddy has no idea if I'm going to bump-and-run it hard or hook it. So it's difficult for a caddie to stand there and tell me it's the wrong club. But he could ask me *how* I'm going to hit it.

I might have a 6-iron and it's 180 yards and I plan to go straight away. If he knows that, he might say, "If you're going straight away, it's not enough club. But if you're going to hit it low and hook it, it's enough club."

I'd like a caddie to get inside me more. I'd like him to say, "I know it's a seven-iron but I want you to take a five-iron and hit it in there low for me." That's a challenge and I like it.

Of course, some players don't want their caddies to help.

Tom Watson and I played a practice round together before the Lancôme in Paris one year. My caddie was an assistant pro from the club, a guy about thirty. I asked him how long he had been there. "Since I was eight years old," he said. I asked him how often he played the course. "Every day," he said. "Good," I said. "You can read the greens for me."

But Tom had another assistant pro caddying for him, and I was standing on the tee when he told him, "I just want you to carry the bag and clean the ball. I don't want you to say anything."

There wasn't any way he was going to beat me on that course. My caddie knew the course so well that I could relax. I won the tournament by five shots.

Tommy Bolt was playing in L.A. and had a caddy who talked a lot, a guy named Snake. Before they teed off, Tommy told him, "Don't say a damn word to me. Even if I ask you something, don't say anything." Well, during the round, Tommy found the ball next to a tree, where you have to hit under a branch, over a lake and onto the green. So Tommy got down there and looked through the trees and sized it up.

"What do you think, Snake?" he asked. "Five-iron?"

"No, Mr. Bolt!" Snake said.

"What do you mean, not a five-iron?" Tommy snorted. "Watch this shot!"

Snake rolled his eyes. "No-o-o, Mr. Bolt!"

But Tommy hit it and the ball stopped about two feet from the hole. He turned to Snake, handed him the 5-iron and said, "Now what the hell do you think about that?"

"Mr. Bolt," Snake said, "that wasn't your ball."

Hey, when those caddies talk, you have to listen to them. But Herman won't say much until after the shot. That's why he's the second-best caddie out there. The best is Golf Ball, who works for Raymond Floyd.

He's a little skinny guy who caddied for Lee Elder for years. He gets inside his player, constantly talking to him, like he's the jockey and you're the horse. He makes you think. He does a great job with Raymond when he's out there, but Golf Ball has pulled an occasional no-show.

The first round at Colonial in 1981 Raymond shot a 66 to take the lead. Next morning we teed off at eight-forty. Golf

Ball wasn't there. Raymond grabbed a substitute caddie but he played poorly. He was about four over par through 16 when we had a rain delay until the next morning. This time Golf Ball showed up. He had worked for Raymond through Florida that spring, when Raymond won back-to-back titles at Doral and the TPC and earned a $200,000 bonus. Golf Ball had a lot of money so he bought a new car, got himself a gal and went out drinking. The next morning the gal and the car were gone and Golf Ball didn't know if he was in Fort Worth or Fort Wayne. Raymond took him back. He's that good.

Herman's a goddamn jewel, though. If I want to practice twelve hours a day, he's right there with me. He's a bachelor. He doesn't drink or run with other caddies. He goes to good motels and gets his own room. He's never given me bad yardage and he never gets in anyone's way. He's very proud of his job and he's independent as hell. He's a lot like me and I think that's one of the reasons we get along so well.

Herman doesn't want to feel indebted to anybody and neither do I. If someone gave me a pair of shoes, a pair of slacks, a golf bag or a club, I'd feel that I had to talk to the guy or have a drink with him or go to his cocktail party. It's my life and I like to be me. I wouldn't obligate myself to anyone if I didn't have anything. When I first moved to El Paso, Martin Lettunich always wanted me to come into the bar and have a beer after we played but I wouldn't go if I didn't have money. Herman's the same way.

Once when we were playing the Nelson Classic in Dallas, I said, "Hey, Herman, why don't you come by my house? I want to show you some clubs."

"No, no," he said, "I ain't got no business there."

"It's just a few minutes from here," I told him.

"I don't need to see any house," he said. "I've seen lots of houses. Lots of clubs, too."

That's how Herman is and I wouldn't trade him for anything in the world. But I wish he'd keep his weight down.

At Memphis in 1979 his brother had to take the bag. Herman's blood pressure was too high and it was too hot there. I thought he was going to have a heart attack. I missed the cut. That's how important a caddie is.

The doctor told Herman if he didn't lose some weight he wasn't going to stay alive very long. That scared him and he lost thirty pounds real quick. After a year, he was feeling better and he put back on not only the thirty pounds but ten more.

We went to Hartford to practice for a week before the U.S. Open in 1980 and Herman damn near bought out the fruit stand across the street from our motel. He'd sit in his room at night watching television and eat six bananas, six apples, six oranges and six pears.

"Herman, just because you're eating fruit, don't think you're going to lose weight," I told him. "That's fattening."

"I ain't believin' you," he said.

"You ever been to the Dallas Zoo?" I asked him.

"Why?" he said.

"Because there's an eight-hundred-pound gorilla there you ought to see," I said. "All they feed that sonuvabitch is fruit and vegetables!"

Herman looked at me real hard. "Boy," he said, "you ain't no good!"

I pay Herman $300 a week plus a percentage—5 percent on a non-win, 10 percent on a victory. He pays his own expenses unless I have to fly cross-country to a tournament. Then I buy his airline ticket. He's just the opposite of Neal in taking care of his money. He always has plenty because he knows I finish playing the U.S. tour the first of October. Then he takes off to L.A. and plays golf the rest of the year.

When I won the Tournament of Champions in 1981, Herman collected $6,900. He had his $300 salary, plus 10 percent of my prize money of $54,000 and a $12,000 bonus Titleist paid me. He took $300 in cash and two checks for $600 each and I sent the other $5,400 to his bank in Memphis. That's a lot of money for a caddie, but a good one is worth every penny.

I pay the same scale around the world. I know how important money is to those guys because I remember making $1.25 for 18 holes. When I got a $10 tip once I figured I could buy a truckload of groceries. That was in 1948, and then you damn near could.

Now it's my turn to make some caddies happy. In South America kids fight over my bag.

In South Africa, a caddie named William Peete works for me. I taught him how to caddie, mapping the course, marking down yardage and all that. The third time he caddied for me I won the Sun City Classic in Bophuthatswana. First money was $18,000 so I gave him $1,800 plus his $300 salary. He'd never seen that much money. He was about my size so I gave him my clothes, too. He wrote me that he bought his mother a house. They don't make anything over there and suddenly they have something. I liked that.

In Japan the women caddies just pull your bag on a cart. They can't communicate with you and they can't give you yardage. You have to do your own homework. In theory all they're supposed to receive is $15 a day from the sponsors. The first time I won $20,000 for third place, I handed my lady ten $100 bills. She looked at me like she couldn't believe it.

And every year on the U.S. tour there's Mister Wonderful again. I've really been lucky to have Herman so long, and maybe he feels the same way about me. I hired him away from Miller Barber at the PGA championship at Congressional. That was Neal Harvey's last tournament with me, and I asked Herman if he wanted the job.

"Oh my God! Oh my God!" he said. "I've always wanted a superstar's bag."

He's a superstar, too, in my book.

Once Cesar Sanudo said, "Herman, how long are you going to caddie for Lee?"

" 'Til death do us part," Herman told him.

No offense, Herman, but I hope you make the first move.

12.
El Paso Exit

By early 1978 my business situation had gone so bad in El Paso that I had to move back to Dallas and start anew. This hurt, because my family and I had some great years in that town.

We had lots of fun and lots of friends in El Paso. I'll always remember Lee Trevino Day there. It was held in the summer of 1971 to celebrate my winning the three Open championships in twenty days. It was a wonderful time, actually a celebration of two cities.

It started with a morning parade through El Paso, which moved across to Juárez. We stopped at the Palacio Municipal, the City Hall, and drank champagne with the mayor, who said some nice things in Spanish. Next was a big civic luncheon in El Paso, a golf exhibition at one of the municipal courses and a big show that night at the Sun Bowl.

That day I already had received plaques, paintings and jewelry. That night they gave me my own street. Yeah, they named one of El Paso's major thoroughfares in my honor. The mayor unveiled a large sign, freshly painted with the new name.

"I really appreciate Lee Trevino Drive," I said. "It's the only street in El Paso I can spell."

I loved El Paso because it was friendly and freewheeling. I could go anywhere, bet and play golf like I always had in the old days.

Once I was in a tough match with Gene Fisher and Bill Eschenbrenner at El Paso Country Club. On 11, I found my ball in a bush 100 yards from the green. The only way I could get it out of there was to hit it left-handed and cut the ball around a tree. So I took a 7-iron, turned the face backward and hit it around the tree and onto the green. Then I sank a 30-foot putt for a birdie. That was good experience. A few weeks later I did the same thing in a Ryder Cup match.

We had lots of fun with trick shots. Bill bet me I couldn't pitch the ball onto an island, make it hit a tree and stay there. If I missed the tree, my ball went into the water. I did it once but he wanted to see it again, so I did it again.

"Want any more of that?" I asked him.

"Naw," he said, "that's it." I won $40 from him.

I had to have an emergency appendectomy while vacationing in New Mexico and I was in a hospital in Truth or Consequences—yeah, that's right, Truth or Consequences, New Mexico. Bill and Frank Redman came to visit me after playing in a tournament in Albuquerque and told me how Frank messed up a bush trying to hit his 4-iron in the backyard of a home by the course. I started laughing and couldn't stop. "If you don't get these guys out of here," I told my nurse, "I'm going to bust open."

For a while I had the British Open trophy in the clubhouse at Horizon Hills. It was in a glass case with some old head covers nobody would buy. Maybe it wasn't an elegant place but it was where my friends could see it.

That was what I loved about El Paso. Nothing fancy there. The attitude was relax, let it be. And that's how it was for years.

Then one day Clyde told me she couldn't get any information about the bonuses I was to receive from contracts with different companies.

I drew an annual salary as head of Lee Trevino Enterprises and the money I earned from golf went into the company. However, the bonuses were to go to me and I paid tax on that money as personal income. Lee Trevino Enterprises had expanded through the years with Don Whittington running the operation as my manager. Martin Lettunich said once, "Hell, Lee has thirty people eating out of his check." This had changed a lot from the days when it was just me, Donnie and Jesse Whittenton, and I said that I wanted them as partners indefinitely.

If I had understood what Martin was saying in my early days out there, I'd be worth $20 million today.

Martin never told me not to do something, but he would say, "Are you sure this is what you want to do?" He was trying to tell me to go slow, be careful.

If I had it to do over, I'd go it alone and stick with Martin's theory of moving slowly and making sound investments. But things started moving too fast and I didn't realize what was best in those days.

Lee Trevino Enterprises had taken a big plunge in the Santa Teresa development in New Mexico, just across the state line from El Paso. Charlie Crowder, the developer who owned the land, had offered me twenty-five choice lots valued at $50,000 each if I would represent his new club. But the company turned it down. Instead, we got the right to operate the club and committed ourselves to finish the golf courses and build the clubhouse. This required heavy financing, but it looked like it could pay off big over the long haul. I also had a big, beautiful house by the 17th fairway. It looked first-class in every way, but we finally found that wasn't what we thought it was either.

My workout room was freezing in wintertime, although we had papers saying the house was fully insulated. "I guarantee you there's no insulation," I said. I punched the wall with my fist and made a big hole. There was nothing inside. Obviously, someone had cut corners at my expense.

Clyde kept going to our office and asking questions about the bonuses but couldn't get any answers. She was frustrated and angry. She wanted to know what was going on in the business, and I did, too.

I began realizing the money wasn't there. Ultimately, the Internal Revenue Service gave me a big surprise—$90,000 worth. The IRS was billing me for additional personal income tax on bonuses that I never received, and subsequently filed a lien against my house.

In the fall of 1977 I asked Frank Redman to join me at the Texas Open in San Antonio. Like a lot of my friends in El Paso, Frank is a first-class guy and a good businessman and I wanted to talk to him.

"I've made five million, but I have only thirty thousand in the bank and I have notes out for almost two million," I said. "Where the hell is my money?"

"Lee," he said, "I think you should get some accountants to find out."

I learned that my bonuses for several years, which amounted to approximately $400,000, had gone back into the company. The company had been pressed for cash, so it had used the bonus money. The company kept getting short-term financing for the Santa Teresa deal while trying to arrange permanent financing, but nothing worked out. The high interest payments ate everything up. It was just a matter of time until we would go under. Since I had given the company management my power of attorney, I could blame no one but myself.

In February of 1978 I met with everyone involved in the deal and told them they weren't getting another damn dime from me. I was going my own way. We started discussing who the hell was going to pay what and one of the bankers jumped up.

"Now wait a minute," he said. "All your contracts, all your insurance policies and all your properties are up for collateral on these notes."

"I understand that," I said, "but I'll tell you one thing you don't control. My putter. Maybe you have my money tied up but you don't control these hands. Either you do it my way or they don't hit the ball."

That banker knew exactly what I was talking about. He sat down.

The bankers wanted to know what we were going to do. "I don't care what you do," I told them. "If you want to go into the golf business, foreclose. I don't have anything. But you've got a golf course out there worth two and a half million and another two million dollars' worth of assets. Now, that's four and a half million for one point nine million I have in notes. If you want to be a golf pro instead of a banker, go out there and run the damn thing. I'm not running it."

They knew exactly where I was coming from then. Of course, financial messes like that one can take a long time to settle. Clyde was determined to move immediately.

She called me while I was playing in the Tucson tournament. "The vans are coming next Wednesday and I'm moving to Dallas," she said. "Do you want to go with me or are you staying here?"

"Hell, no, take my stuff with you," I said. I told her that after I played in Phoenix the next week I would fly straight to Dallas.

She hired two long moving vans, had our cars and all our furniture loaded into them and took off for Dallas. It takes a lot of nerve for a person to do that.

I finished fourth in Tucson and won $10,000. In Phoenix I was second and won $27,000. By then our bank account was down to $8,000 and we needed that $37,000 badly. I told Clyde there was no way I was sending that money to the company.

They gave me some heat from El Paso, claiming that money should go into the company. I said I wasn't giving it up. "If you guys want to go to court and see what the judge says," I told them, "that's up to you."

In Dallas we lived with the Salinas family until we moved into our own house in April. We set up Lee Trevino Enterprises in a new office with me, Clyde, and Arnold and Albert Salinas running it. Arnold and Albert handled the day-to-day details of the business, with Clyde overseeing things while I got busy trying to win more money on the tour.

I had one of my best years to that point, winning $228,723 and finishing sixth on the money list. In 1979 I climbed to $238,732 and fourth, and in 1980 I hit a new peak, $385,814, while finishing second and winning my fifth Vardon Trophy. My stroke average of 69.73 for 82 rounds was the lowest on the tour since Sam Snead's 69.23 in 1950. And I did it when I was forty years old.

But by then I felt a lot younger than I had when we were struggling with the financial problems in El Paso. It was almost the end of 1978 before I managed to break the logjam.

In late November my lawyer told me that if we didn't settle the thing before the first of the year it was going to cost me another $65,000 in income tax. I'd had enough. Charlie Crowder, the owner of Santa Teresa, had pretty well stayed out of it, but I called and told him I was going to sue him and everybody else—the bankers, the CPAs, the club members—if it wasn't settled in a week.

He didn't want a lawsuit because that would lock everything up at Santa Teresa, and he couldn't sell land or houses.

Well, pretty soon the problem was settled. Charlie took over all the notes and I was released from all obligations.

Eventually he bought Jesse and Donnie out of the golf operation.

All I wound up with was two acres of commercial real estate in the middle of El Paso worth about $300,000, some tax credits and my contracts. But I had my independence and that was important.

Everything has gone well since we moved back to Dallas. The best thing that ever happened to Clyde and me was getting away from everyone and taking over our entire business. It has brought us a lot closer. I think this was what she wanted from Day One, because she likes to be involved and she does make good decisions. It's amazing how she has learned tax shelters and real estate.

While I'm not worth $20 million, I've managed to generate a lot of revenue since we settled in Dallas. My foreign tournaments became lucrative with sponsors willing to pay me $40,000 or $50,000 a week appearance money in addition to whatever I win, plus expenses and first-class travel for two. I have a heavy schedule of exhibitions at $20,000 a day. I've added some very good contracts with outstanding companies like Coors beer, Bridgestone tires and Rawlings golf company. And I've got a contract with La Cita golf course and condominium development in Titusville, Florida.

I've learned a lesson from all this, and maybe it will help some other guy who finds himself making big money in golf or football or baseball or some other sport. Now I hire the best accountants and attorneys and listen to their advice before making a decision. Just stick with them and don't try to get rich overnight. This knowledge has served me well these last few years in Dallas, even if I paid a tremendous price to learn it.

I miss a lot of the life and people in El Paso but I'm glad Clyde ordered those moving vans when she did.

13.
Let My People Glow

I was walking to the 18th tee, ready to finish a practice round before the 1981 PGA championship at Atlanta
Athletic Club, and the gallery was all around me. "I got a
joke to tell," I said. Everyone moved a little closer.

"There's these three guys in a bar—an Irishman, an Italian
and a Mexican—and they're all trying to outdo each other.
The Irishman says, 'I'll take an IW.' And the bartender says,
'What's an IW?'

" 'Irish Whiskey,' the Irishman says.

"So then the Italian says, 'I'll take an IWW.'

"And the bartender says, 'What's that?'

"And the Italian says, 'Italian white wine.'

"Now the Mexican gets up there and he's gonna try to
outdo 'em all. So he says, 'I'll take a fifteen.'

"And the bartender says, 'What the hell is that?'

"And the Mexican says, 'A Seven-and-Seven.' "

They loved it. I did, too. I feed off people. Sometimes I

think the fans follow me as much to hear me talk as to watch me play. Whatever, I'm the people's champion and proud of it. But this can cause problems.

I'm public property. I've created that by having a happy-go-lucky personality. But I can't stay open for business twenty-four hours a day. I need time to myself like any human being. That's why I've become a hermit on the road, watching TV and ordering room service instead of going out for dinner and drinks.

I give it a thousand percent when I'm out there. When I get out of that car at the course, I'm on stage. I'm the Muhammad Ali of the tour. Well, maybe I'm more than that.

I've been with Muhammad Ali on a few occasions, on talk shows and such. You can sit with him backstage and he never says a word. But as soon as he walks out and the camera goes on, he goes into his act.

Well, mine is not an act. I *enjoy* what I do. But I can't do it around the clock.

I think deep down every person has a certain amount of rebel in him, and somewhere down the line he wants to bring that rebel out. A lot of people don't do it because of their upbringing, but they enjoy watching someone who does.

Just because I'm the player of the people the fans feel they can walk over, shake hands and start talking to me in the middle of dinner. I'm as friendly as the next guy, but frankly, this has gotten to be too much. Particularly the night a man sat down, pushed my plate aside to get my autograph and shoved Clyde's food into her lap.

Back in the days when I was busy checking out the top 10,000 bars in the United States, I was enjoying a few drinks one evening when a beautiful girl moved in beside me.

"You're Lee Trevino, aren't you?"

"Yes I am." Hell, I would have told her I was Fidel Castro if that was who she was looking for.

"Oh, I've always admired you," she said. "Will you do something for me?"

"Certainly," I said. I figured she wanted me to come to her table and meet someone.

"Would you sign this five-dollar bill for me?"

Hey, I was impressed. I laughed and took that bill and signed it, "To Pat. Super Mex, Lee Trevino, 1973." I handed it to her and she clutched it.

"Oh, I'll cherish this all my life," she said. "I'll never spend this."

Well, at midnight I paid the check with a $50 bill and got that $5 bill in my change. She forgot to add, "Unless I get thirsty."

Next day at the golf course a kid came up to me with a gum wrapper to sign. "Son, I've got something special for you," I said. "Here's an autographed five-dollar bill."

Those are the funny times. Some autograph-seekers can be pretty tough on your body and your clothes.

I've been stuck by pens and left bleeding. Once a lady cut my hand with the sharp end of a combination pen and letter opener. Maybe she thought it was an envelope.

When leisure suits were in style I had a white one I wore with a turquoise necklace and choke collar. I was coming out of the clubhouse during the Tokai tournament in Japan and the fans caught me. I stood in the middle of all these people who were holding little boards and wide felt-tip pens. They wanted my autograph on something they could frame.

When I finished, I looked like a zebra. I had marks all over my stomach, back and arms.

After so many years of being interrupted during my meal to go over and meet Uncle George or sign Junior's napkin, I started staying in. This isn't the way I want it. I would like to go out for every meal when I'm on the road, but I've found I can't even go into the hotel coffee shop for breakfast without people coming by. Don't get me wrong. They're fans and that's great, but sometimes you wish they would just let you have some time for yourself.

I hate ordering room service every day. I don't think I'd

have the weight problem I do if I wasn't eating in front of a television set all the time. You can't get the wide choice of food in your room that you can on the restaurant menu.

Some hotels are very considerate and fix me food not listed on the room service menu, like spinach salad. This helps sometimes, but there's still the basic problem of eating in the room. I eat and I lie down immediately. No exercise.

Once I would have choked to death in my room at the World Series of Golf if Albert Salinas hadn't been there.

I love fruit and I had ordered cantaloupe. I cut a slice, took a big bite and it stuck in my throat. Albert was lying on the bed and I couldn't say a word. I couldn't spit it out, I couldn't swallow it. I couldn't breathe. So I hit Albert on the leg. He looked up and I pointed at my throat. My God, his eyes got big as saucers.

He grabbed my stomach and tried to pull in and force me to cough, but my stomach was so tight he couldn't do anything. So he took his fist and hit me in the back. He almost knocked me down, but the jolt made me swallow it. I could breathe but tears were rolling down my cheeks. Albert started laughing and all I could do was gasp, "My God!"

Now I'm very careful about what I eat in my room. I'll usually have fish or chicken. If I have steak, I cut it into very small cubes, just like I do with all my cantaloupe.

Now, let's talk about someone else for a while. You want to know the five greatest golfers I've ever seen? In order, they are Jack Nicklaus, Ben Hogan, Sam Snead, Tommy Bolt (surprised?) and Arnold Palmer. I'll tell you why.

Nicklaus has to be the all-time best. He has all that talent plus a tremendous grasp of the game of golf. When he turned pro in 1962 he took a more scientific approach. He started pacing the courses, writing down yardage from key points he needed to know to help him make the right shots during his round. All of those players back in the 1940s and 1950s played by eyesight. Nicklaus was the first to chart courses . . .

knowing how far you hit a 9-iron, an 8-iron, a 7-iron. Then when he got out on the course he looked at a tree or the back of a bunker or a sprinkler as a checkpoint, and knew how far it was to the edge of the green. Attention to detail is what helped him emerge as the greatest player.

For a lot of years when he won so much he still had his critics. First, I believe it was because he knocked off the King of the Hill, Palmer, who is the sport's all-time hero. They resented him and called him Ohio Fats. Arnold always has been an attractive athlete and Jack was a bulgy kid with a crewcut. Then, they said he was too wild with his drives. Well, let me tell you something. You don't win nineteen major championships and finish second in twenty-nine more hitting that thing crooked. Now so much has changed. Jack is trim and handsome with his shaggy blond hair and he's a big favorite. I'm glad.

He's helped me a great deal, but he likes to do a little needling like anyone else. We teed off together in the Tournament of Champions and I hit a little driver down the middle of the fairway and he hit his in the rough. We're walking along and I said, "Boy, I'm driving this ball straight." Jack looked at me and said, "I could hit a five-iron in the fairway." Meaning that I didn't drive it any farther than he would have hit his 5-iron. Well, we went on and he had one of his worst days. I shot 67 and he shot 80. We walked off 18 to our cart and he sat there shaking his head.

I said, "You know what you should have done today, don't you?"

"What's that?" he asked.

"You should have driven with your five-iron."

Jack grinned. "I had that coming," he said.

I've always been his number-one fan. We come from completely different backgrounds, but what we have in common is respect. That's what is so great about this game. People don't look at you and think about where you came from as a young man. Judgment Day is *now.* It's what you can do with those fourteen golf clubs.

Hogan is my second choice for the greatest players. I had the pleasure of playing with him in the Houston tournament at Champions in 1970. He was retired from active competition and hadn't entered a tournament since the 1967 U.S. Open, but the man could still play. We were paired in the final round and he began the day four shots out of the lead, and birdied four of the first seven holes. His ball always went straight to the flag. Then he tired on the back nine and his game slipped. This man must have been unbelieveable when he was out there all the time.

He was notorious for never talking when he played, but he talked with me a lot. I've visited him at his office in Fort Worth and I have an open invitation to come over to Shady Oaks and play with him. "Just call me," he said.

I doubt you could fill a foursome with the people he's invited for a game, so that was gratifying to me.

Even more than Nicklaus, Hogan spent a tremendous amount of time concentrating on golf. He practiced like he was driven by demons. In the late 1940s and early 1950s, there wasn't as much commercialism in the game as there is today. I don't know if Hogan would have been a commercial item, or if he would have wanted to devote time and energy to advertising and appearances. Hogan believed he was as good as he was because he spent so much time at his trade, shutting out everything else.

Hogan believed golf is a game of close misses. He said not once will you hit the ideal shot. He believed the guy who consistently came close to ideal shots in a golf tournament will win a helluva lot of money. He impressed me tremendously, both in his play and his philosophy.

One day I went over to see him at his equipment company. "Well, what can I do for you?" he said. So I told him, "Ben, I'm putting terrible." I was just hoping I could get back in his private bin and he'd give me a special putter. "I'm having a helluva time," I said. "Do you have any putters?"

And just that quick he responded, "We don't make putters."

And that was it. I mean, case closed.

His right-hand man, Chip Bridges, was there, and Chip said, "What he's trying to tell you is he doesn't make them because he doesn't like any of them. They look bad, and Ben feels no one would buy a putter with his name on it anyway."

That made sense. Putting was the one bad part of Ben's game, and we just ended up laughing about it.

My number-three man, Snead, is a fantastic athlete. Here's a man who at sixty-seven shot his age in a PGA tournament! That's like bringing Joe DiMaggio out of retirement and seeing him go 4–for–4.

Flexibility is what has kept Sam in the game so long. He has a terrific pair of legs. He's double-jointed. He can stand flat-footed in a room and kick an eight-foot ceiling. If you don't believe it, bet him some time. I've seen him do it a half dozen times.

He can still play. It's amazing what he can do. He was an exceptionally long hitter and that's what helped him as he got older. He can still hit the ball as far as some of the shorter hitters on the tour. He must have been incredible back in the 1930s and then after the war. I don't know the records but he probably beat Hogan as much as Hogan beat him.

He probably didn't spend as much time on his game as Hogan did, though. Sam was more outgoing. He had more fun. If he had spent more time on his game, he probably would have won more majors. He might even have won the U.S. Open, which somehow always got away from him. But then, a lot of us can't kick the ceiling.

My fourth choice, Bolt, probably has left more money on the golf course than anyone in history. I've played with him a lot in his later years and it's phenomenal what he can do with a golf ball. He's probably a better striker of the ball than

Nicklaus, Hogan and Snead. He has a tremendous feel with his clubs and a great sense of depth. He can hit a ball so many distances and so many ways.

The only thing wrong with Tommy is his temper. That's probably why he won only one major championship. After he won the U.S. Open at Southern Hills in 1958, he was practicing for another tournament and didn't like his shot to the green. He hit a second ball and then a third, and a PGA official reminded him there was a fine of $25 per extra ball hit to the green.

Tommy glared at the official a second, then threw a $100 bill on the grass. "Keep the change," he said. "I'm going to hit two more." People have told me he withdrew from many tournaments where he was leading or one shot out. He'd get mad at somebody or the course or a shot that didn't go right and just pick up and leave. That's something you can't take away from a person. If that's how he chose to behave, that's his right.

But I have one especially fond memory of playing with Tommy. I think I set the record for beer-drinking while playing an exhibition with him at Gary, Indiana: thirteen on the back nine. To this day people are still trying to break that record. Just try to go out and play nine holes and drink thirteen beers.

I started drinking them because I shot 30 on the front nine and had Tommy by about eight shots. I hit the ball over the green on the last hole, a par-5. I chili-dipped it twice, but got it on the green and made 6, and I think Tommy won the exhibition by a shot. I believe I shot 43.

Palmer is my fifth choice because he was such an outstanding player in his prime and has made a tremendous contribution to the game. Arnold made millions of people really notice what we're doing out there on the tour. He generated great business opportunities for the sport.

He was famous for his charges in a tournament, and he lived and died by them. He was aggressive. He might be leading by one or two shots but he wouldn't be cautious. He'd go for the flag from the middle of an alligator's back.

Arnold was everyone's hero, a common guy who hitched his pants and let his shirttail flap in the breeze, a man who came from behind to win. When he was really doing his thing back there in the 1960s he had a tremendous influence on players out on the tour. When Arnold Palmer's name went up on the board everybody got nervous, and rightfully so. They knew he was going to make a charge because that was his style. People loved it, but this probably hurt Arnold's game as much as it helped him.

He won eighty tournaments around the world, but he probably lost as many because of the way he played. It left him open to big mistakes, big setbacks. But that's what the public wanted. They always went for The Bomb, even if it blew up in his face from time to time.

Bobby Jones? I never saw him play except in some old films. He had to be a terrific player in his era, but it's difficult for me to say just how good he was. You have to consider the equipment he used: light-weighted clubs, very little steel, wooden shafts. I do remember Hogan mentioning that Bobby Jones hooked the ball badly. When steel shafts were introduced back in the early 1930s he hooked even worse, simply because there was no torque in the shaft. A wooden shaft has a little torque in it. I don't know how well Jones would have competed against today's players, but he would have looked great out there in his knickers.

Tom Watson doesn't have a long enough track record to be measured against the all-time greats yet. You need fifteen years for that. There are more distractions for Tom and there's more topflight competition. Today you may be playing great and some player who's never won a tournament can come out of the pack and beat you.

But I believe Tom will take Nicklaus' place one of these days. He's that good. He's got Nicklaus' disposition. He trains like Nicklaus. He thinks like Nicklaus. He goes straight forward and doesn't let a bad shot upset him.

Everyone raves about Tom being a great putter, and he is, but they may not appreciate the rest of his game. He has to be doing something right to get the ball across that other 450 yards from tee to green.

I've known Ben Crenshaw since he was fifteen, when he caddied for Hal Underwood in a tournament in Texas. I've always wondered if he might someday be a true superstar. He has talent, and with his soft-spoken personality he'd give the tour a real shot in the arm if he won a major championship.

Crenshaw and Watson have perfect golf bodies: strong legs, strong arms, strong shoulders, flat bellies, good hands and the right height, about five nine. Ben's problem is his wildness with his driver. It catches up with him in a crucial round, like it did in the third round of the 1981 British Open, when he shot 76 to Bill Rogers' 67 and blew himself out of contention. But he may win the Masters some day because you don't have to drive it so straight there.

He's very popular with the players. He amused everyone before the final round of the British Open a few years ago, running up and down the hall asking if anyone had a blow-dryer.

"A what?" I said.

"Man, I've got to blow my hair dry or I've got to withdraw from the tournament," Ben said. "I don't play anywhere unless I can blow my hair dry."

Bill Rogers is another one with a good game and a great personality. Hey, when ol' Buck smiles, he really means it. For years he never got the attention he deserved, and then he won the British Open. It's going to be interesting to see how he holds up over the long haul.

Bill is thin, and I don't know if he has the stamina to keep up the pace that I have for so many years. But he hits the ball awfully straight and he's a competitor. He gets mad, but he gets mad at himself. And that's good. Bill is a young Don

January—tall, lanky, great touch. He'll play as long as he wants to play.

Crenshaw running around looking for a hair-dryer was really funny. I just wish we saw some humor in more of the young players. Humor is pretty rare on the golf tour now. There aren't many of us who will stop between holes to tell a joke anymore.

I believe my sense of humor comes out because I'm the last of the club pros who turned touring professional. It used to be a lot of fun out there because 96 to 98 percent of the pros once had club jobs. They were salesmen with a gift for gab. They'd go out, play in a few tournaments, then go home and sell some shoes and golf balls. They were attuned to serving the public.

You have to be a salesman in that pro shop. You have to give your members a little humor. Tell them a few jokes, laugh with them, even if it's for just five minutes. A member will buy more from a golf pro if he likes him. You're there not only to promote the game but also to make that guy forget his work at the office, forget a bad marriage, forget an illness. For that one little moment you give him in the pro shop, when you're laughing and giggling and raising hell, you're someone special to that member. And that's what the pros used to do.

So many pro golfers today have gone from high school to college to the tour. They have been totally isolated. They've never had to deal with the public. They didn't have to sell shoes or golf balls or figure out how to make some guy happy.

Maybe it's because of their background, but a lot of these young players are conservative. Oh, I guess there's nothing wrong with that. If I were, I'd probably have twice as much money today. With me, it's been easy come, easy go. Maybe these youngsters don't have that attitude. Maybe they don't feel as secure as I do, don't have the confidence in their ability to make as much money as I make.

There are some exceptions on the tour today. Fuzzy Zoeller came out loud, half crazy. His winning the Masters was one of the greatest things that ever happened. Hubert Green won the U.S. Open and he'll talk to a tree, like me. He'd be happy in a closet with a six-pack of beer. Chi Chi Rodriguez has great rapport with the people, but he's older than I am.

It's fun remembering old times, but there's no way life out there now can be like it used to be. Now it's a business, pure and simple, and when their round is over these young guys vanish.

A pro used to bring a sports coat, white shirt and tie to the tournament and hang them in his locker because during the day some member might say, "Hey, you want to have dinner with us tonight?"

So the pro hit some practice balls after the round, took a quick shower, put the same trousers back on, slipped on that white shirt, tie and coat and got a free meal. That was important. Those guys were living four, five, six to a room and sweating out every nickel. Today we go to a tournament and a guy may get a suite for himself!

It's really different now. I'm one of the last guys out there who sold equipment and gave lessons. But I'm glad I did.

The seniors tournaments, for players over fifty, have become popular the last few years, but I think we need an over-forty tour—for guys who can still play a little better than seniors and are funny. Of course, eventually it would get just like the regular tour is now. These twenty-eight-year-olds are going to turn forty some day. All these dull young players will get old.

Well, whatever it is, one of these days I won't be playing out there anymore. What'll I do then? I'm going to start smoking a pipe, get me some gray flannel trousers, a white shirt, a red, white and blue striped tie, and a blue blazer. Then I'm going to get a can of dandruff and become a USGA official.

Between rulings, of course, I'll still tell a few jokes.

14.
Special Times, Special People

I had another joke during that PGA championship in Atlanta in 1981, but this one was on me. I forgot to sign my scorecard.

I learned about it thirty minutes after I finished the first round. I was in the clubhouse, drinking a beer and wisecracking with some writers about losing four strokes in the last three holes and finishing with a 74. I remembered how I had shot 73 in the first round at Tanglewood in 1974 and still won the PGA. I thought there was a chance I might come back again. Well, I did until Tom Weiskopf tapped me on the shoulder and asked to speak with me privately.

I slid my chair back and stood up. "As big as he is," I said, "I better follow him."

Tom's face never was longer. I couldn't figure what was troubling him because he was in good spirits when he, Lanny Wadkins and I played.

"Lee, I'm sorry but there was a mistake in the scorer's tent," he told me. "I signed your card as well as my own and your score went in without your signature. I'm afraid you've been disqualified."

In all my years in golf that was one thing I had never done. I guess you're never too old to screw up, though. I was out and Tom felt terrible about it. I told him not to worry. What happened was my fault. I broke a rule and I was out.

I went back to my table, got another beer and thought about my weird year in America's three major championships for 1981.

In April, I arrived at the Masters after a terrible experience at Titusville, Florida, where I tried to revive Ed Parkin, one of my partners in the country club–condominium complex there. Ed suffered a heart attack and was lying on the floor in his condo when I started giving him mouth-to-mouth resuscitation while Arnold Salinas worked on his chest. It was hopeless. He must have been dead when we got to him.

Ed was a small guy, a little older than me, and he stayed in good condition. He was wearing running shorts, T-shirt, sneakers and headband, so it looked like he had just come in from jogging. And then he was gone.

I didn't sleep my first two nights in Augusta. I started having chest pains and my arm felt numb. It was all a state of mind but I couldn't just shake it off. I actually was playing well but you couldn't tell it by what I did at Augusta National. I shot 77–77 and missed the cut.

In June, we played the U.S. Open at Merion, where I beat Jack Nicklaus in our playoff in 1971. But now I'd had a thirty-one-day layoff from competitive golf because of back trouble. I didn't know where the ball was going. I shot 72–76 and missed the cut again.

Now my PGA mistake left me with a record in the U.S. majors of cut-cut-no signature. Hey, I was on a roll.

"It's one of those years," I told the writers. "Jimmy Carter had four of 'em, so I don't feel so bad."

Here's what happened in the scoring tent at the PGA when we came off the 18th green:

There were three chairs across the table from the PGA officials. Wadkins came in first and sat down in the chair on the right. He had kept my scorecard so he signed to attest it, then slid it to his left, in front of the empty middle chair. When Weiskopf sat down in that chair, Wadkins really didn't think about it. He figured I'd get my card.

But Weiskopf just signed the card without looking at it, something he said he always did. Then I sat down beside him and I had his card. It was pretty confusing in the tent—a lot of talk and people asking if we wanted cold drinks. I had made an error on his score, giving him a 4 on Number 9 instead of a 3. While we corrected that, the fact that Weiskopf had signed another card was forgotten.

A PGA official saw him sign that first card and picked it up. In a minute, I asked him, "Where's my card?" He shoved it across to me. When I saw two signatures on it, I shoved it back. I don't know why. Tom's signature sure doesn't look like mine. Then the official pushed it toward me again.

"Did you shoot seventy-four?" he asked me. "What's par?" I said. I thought it was seventy-one but he told me it was seventy. So I said, "seventy-four is right. I shot four over." So I had a second look at the card and still didn't see what was wrong.

Later that official said he just checked the cards for two signatures because you can't read the names most of the time anyway. I didn't blame him for anything, either. It was my responsibility and I blew it.

They caught the error when Weiskopf went back to the tent and told the PGA rules chairman, Bill Clarke, that he was confused about signing a card that had my score on it but not my signature. Clarke found my card and then they saw the error.

Funny thing, hundreds of fans were walking around the course with copies of my card showing Weiskopf's signature on the contestant's line because the PGA made copies of all players' cards and gave them away for souvenirs. None of them had noticed it, either.

If Weiskopf hadn't caught it, it might have gone unnoticed until after the tournament. But if I had come back like I did in 1974 and won the championship, I wouldn't have accepted the trophy or the money. I was guilty, and that was it.

I was just sorry to see Weiskopf so upset by it. I really like him. He has tremendous talent, but he's his own worst enemy. He had the ability that Nicklaus had but not the determination and patience. He had a great year in 1973, winning the British Open and four tournaments on the U.S. tour, but in 1974 he walked off the course at five or six tournaments.

He came up in the shadow of Nicklaus, playing at Ohio State a couple of years after Jack. When he joined the tour I think Jack's great reputation bothered him. The only time his attitude toward Jack really showed was when Tom was winning a lot. We'd be on the practice tee and he'd say, "Where's Nicklaus? Bring that son of a gun on. I can beat him any time he gets on the golf course."

Now that's the attitude he should always have. That's the attitude that has helped me win. But he went into slumps and he wasn't aggressive. He feels very strongly about his way of life, though.

"I want to be myself," he said. "I don't want to be like someone else and I don't want people to say what I should be. This is my life and nobody else's, and to me golf is not everything in the world. If I want to quit in the middle of the golf course, I'm going to quit."

But sometimes he couldn't understand why players with less ability did better than he did. During the U.S. Open at Cherry Hills in 1978 he looked at the leader board, saw who was ahead at the time, and shook his head.

"Now I can't believe that," he told me. "I can spot that guy three shots a round. I don't understand it."

"Tom," I said, "he's not *supposed* to beat you and you *can* give him three shots, but he's got everything under control. When something goes bad, he fights back."

Tom has everything he needs to be a great golfer. He must be six three or so, and I believe he's the best of the players taller than six two. He has the power, the distance, the swing; but he needs Nicklaus' attitude. It's not too late for him because with his wiry, flexible body he'll be able to compete against the young guys until he's in his middle fifties.

I hope his best years are ahead of him. But I know whenever I play with him I'll be damn sure I sign my scorecard.

I'm a lucky guy. Even in the off years, good things happen. The week after missing the cut at the Masters, I won the Tournament of Champions, my first victory in California in sixteen years of playing there. And late in 1981 I scored another very important first. I won in Japan.

I was anxious to get to La Costa for the Tournament of Champions. I've always loved a challenge. It inspires me to hear people say I can't do something, and there had to be plenty of them saying I couldn't win anything after I shot those two 77s at Augusta. But I knew I was playing well. I'm my own guy and you can't get inside me. At La Costa I put everything out of my mind and just played.

After nearly everything had gone wrong one week, nearly everything went right the next. I even had a dream the night before the first round that I birdied the first four holes, and I did. By the final round I had a one-shot lead over Raymond Floyd and I was feeling great.

I came out to the first tee on Sunday morning and saw my old pal, Lester Nehamkin, a big guy who shoots photos at a lot of tournaments. You couldn't miss him. He was wearing a little umbrella for a hat, orange pants, some flowery shirt from Hawaii that he kept unbuttoned and underneath a T-shirt with "Fruit of the Loom" written across the chest.

That T-shirt was big enough to put one of my cars in, so I grabbed the front, stretched it out and got in it with him.

We stood there wearing the same T-shirt with two heads sticking out and the other photographers had a great time with us.

Raymond and I had a minute before we teed off, and I noticed blackbirds all around trying to get worms out of the ground for their breakfast. I chased them 40 yards down the first tee before I got them to fly off.

I shot 34 on the front nine, but Raymond shot 33 to tie me. We had a 7-shot lead on the field, so on the back nine it became strictly match play. It was like old times at Horizon Hills when the cotton farmers bet on me and the Tenison crowd had their money on Raymond. I was watching what he was doing and he was watching what I was doing. It was fun because Raymond and I always have had the utmost respect for each other.

I saved myself with a 25-foot birdie putt on 12 when he was standing there waiting to make a 4-footer, then he hit into the highest rough on the course on 13 and wound up with a bogey. I left an 8-iron four feet from the hole for a birdie, so I walked off 13 with a 2-shot lead. After he bogeyed 15, I felt I had it under control. The three closing holes are extremely tough ones, but I wasn't scared of bogeying all three and I doubted he could birdie more than one.

Raymond and I shook hands when it was over, but this time all I had to do was accept the trophy and a check for $54,000. Somebody else put the carts away that evening.

On Thanksgiving Day I teed off in the Casio Cup, a new tournament for me in one of my favorite countries, Japan. I love to play there because the people are crazy about golf and I have great rapport with them. I'm dark-complexioned and I'm their size.

But for all my commercial success and popularity I never had won a tournament in Japan until I took the Casio. That made it very pleasant, and profitable. First prize paid $50,-000, and I also made a bundle in a match before the tournament. I got home just in time to celebrate my forty-second birthday and have a wisdom tooth pulled. Even when my jaw was numb with Novocaine I felt like smiling and bowing toward the East.

My sombrero logo is a familiar sight in Japan. I had a ten-year, million-dollar contract with a manufacturer marketing a full line of sports clothes and accessories that was so successful the company came back to discuss extending my deal. Now the company has expanded the line and you can find my sombrero on umbrellas, hats, blankets, cigarette lighters, purses, wallets and belts. And they're all expensive, first-class items.

I did a New Year's Eve television show with a comedian and a boxer there once. I wore a kimono and shoes with my toes sticking out, and we bowed to each other, spoke a little Japanese, hit a few balls in a driving contest and then had a hole-in-one contest. It was a blast.

Aside from all the fun and money that can be had in Japan, it's nice that the country's top world-class player, Isao Aoki, and I have a lot in common.

He came from a humble background, growing up on a farm, and he started playing golf at a very young age. He's a perfect example of a Lee Trevino when it comes to a golf swing. He doesn't have that classic look, either. He and I are walking proof that it doesn't take a beautiful swing to play good golf.

He breaks all the rules when it comes to playing bunker shots. He's very wristy when he's chipping and putting. When he hits a golf ball he falls away from it. He's not a picture of the perfect golfer but he knows exactly where the thing is going. That's the secret to good golf. I guarantee you Mr. Aoki can play his pill.

I just wish I still had the type of putting stroke he uses. I'm not talking about putting the putter up on the heel like he does, but the hand action. A lot of U.S. players used to have it, but now we've gotten so mechanical with our putting that we use too many moving parts—our shoulders and arms —and we don't break our wrists.

My first few years I was very wristy. I kept my arms close to the body and let my hands do it all. Then I started trying to work the putter on a straight line and became too mechanical. That way I have more moving parts, and more pressure to hit it.

I look at Aoki putting and remember how it was. There are days that man is uncanny on the greens. I just wish I could putt that way again.

Just northwest of South Africa, about two hours from Johannesburg, you'll find one helluva golf course. Gary Player designed it and Sol Kerzner, who operates the Sun City hotel and casino, built it. There's a game preserve around the course and you'll usually see some rhinos and ostriches during your round, and a family of baboons will jump the fence and come over to drink from the lake. The hotel is beautiful and the casino is as great as anything you'll see in Las Vegas. It's a wonderful place to celebrate the New Year, especially when you're playing golf's first million-dollar tournament.

So I greeted 1982 in Bophuthatswana, a small country with an all-black government that has benefited from Sol Kerzner's spectacular promotions at Sun City. He's the guy who paid Frank Sinatra $1.9 million for nine shows, heavyweight Mike Weaver $1 million for a fight and spread all that dough around for five golfers in the Sun City Challenge. Sol is a few years older than me and he's a beautiful man. He wasn't ringing his bell or flying his flag. He simply was very sincere about promoting worldwide attention to Sun City and making money for Bophuthatswana. Since half of the fees and purses he paid for these big events went in taxes to that poor country, Sol did a swell job.

I had won the Sun City Classic there eleven months before and earned $18,000, but this time I made $110,000—before the tax collector got his cut. And that was for finishing fourth.

I shot 70 in the first round, but the next day I did something I'd never done before—3-putted each of the first three holes. I didn't play too well after that but I still had a wonderful time, including watching Johnny Miller and Seve Ballesteros shoot it out for nine holes in a sudden-death playoff.

Nicklaus, who bogeyed the last hole to miss the playoff, earned $130,000 for third and Player, who had so much to do with creating the whole thing, got $100,000 for fifth.

Gary had been struggling with his game for a long time but he still could give an event a touch of class. He's smaller than me and maybe four years older, so it really was no surprise that he couldn't be a champion golfer forever. His physical limitations finally hurt his game. But for a lot of years he did a great job, flying back and forth from Johannesburg and winning all over the world.

Gary always put the fear of God in me because he's such a competitor. He never gives up. I don't care if he's lying 8 in the middle of the fairway, 150 yards from the cup. He's looking at his scorecard. He wants to know where the flag is and he's trying to hole the damn thing for a 9.

Some American players have been jealous of him and his success in our country, but a lot of people don't remember that he donated his entire $25,000 purse to cancer research and junior golf when he won the U.S. Open at Bellerive in 1965.

He's a fine designer of golf courses, too. I believe Gary has a great future in that field because he laid out a perfect course the first time at Sun City. It's rare when even the best courses don't need some changes. Nicklaus designed a beauty with his Muirfield Village in Ohio, but he still had to go back and rebuild some bunkers.

It was a kick to be out on that course simply as a spectator, watching Miller and Seve go after it for nine holes, first one and then the other hitting a great shot or making a pressure putt to stay even. That playoff was the most exciting thing I've ever seen. I've only left the clubhouse to watch two other tournaments, the 1963 PGA that Nicklaus won at Dallas Athletic Club and the finish of the Tom Watson–Nicklaus final round of the 1977 British Open at Turnberry, but I stayed out for all nine holes of this one.

When Miller left a 30-foot putt just six inches short and then putted out, I guess Seve had had enough. He had to make a 5-footer to tie, but his ball stopped eight or ten inches short. By then it was almost dark and they were just drained from playing so long. But the money—a difference of $340,-000 between first and second—made it worthwhile.

Miller won $500,000, or $250,000 for himself and $250,-000 for the Bophuthatswana government, and I admire him for coming back as a top player after a long slump. He was the Golden Boy of the mid-1970s and he never should have been bothered by hearing people describe him as tall and skinny. Actually, he was big enough, but he messed himself up with a weight program, adding some bulk he didn't need. That cost him his swing and his confidence.

A lot of players never regain those, but as the shadows of the mountains stretched across the course that evening, it looked like Miller had.

As for me, I was drunk before they teed off on the last hole of the playoff. I'd already had a dozen beers watching them play and then Sol was so excited he said, "This is the greatest thing that could have happened. We need champagne!"

In a minute one of his lieutenants came running back with some Dom Perignon. So we were out there, whooping and laughing, passing that champagne around and drinking it out of the bottle like a bunch of rednecks.

Presentations were a lot of fun, too.

Sol's wife is a beautiful young lady who was Miss World and Miss South Africa and she passed out the prize money. When she gave me my check for $110,000 she kissed me.

"Honey," I said, "if you kiss me again I'll give you this check back!"

The way Clyde looked at me, she must have wondered if I thought I was invisible again. Hell, I was just enjoying myself.

In fact, I enjoyed myself so much that night that I gave up cigarettes the next day. I sat up with Sol in the lounge until six in the morning, drinking red wine and smoking fifteen packs. Sean Connery and his wife, Micheline, were going to play golf with Clyde and Arnold Salinas and I was going to keep score. But when I got out of bed I couldn't talk. My throat was hurting bad. I vowed to Clyde on the spot, "I'll never smoke another one."

I took a drag on my first one when I was ten so thirty-two years of cigarettes was enough.

A good example of the difference in the generations in my family is the style of transportation. When I was a little boy I came to town in a Model A Ford. My kids ride to school in a Cadillac.

Except Ricky. He lives in Pensacola, Florida, with his mother and I gave him a car for Christmas when he was seventeen.

I've always tried to provide for him just like I would if he lived with me. I'm just sorry we haven't spent too much time together. When he was about two his mother married a man who was attending morticians' school in Dallas, and when he graduated they moved to Columbia, Missouri. They divorced, married each other again, divorced again and then Linda married a Navy man. She and I are very good friends and have been for years. After both of us remarried, we became human again.

Ricky did live with Clyde and me for about a year in El Paso but he didn't like it when we disciplined him and he moved back with his mother when he was fifteen. I believe he had been living like I did at that age, running around with older kids and doing what he liked. We shot some pool and I could tell from watching his bridge that he had been hanging around pool halls and probably drinking a few beers for some time.

When he graduated from high school I felt very proud. He was the first member of my family to do it. He wasn't real excited about going to college but I pushed that just like I am with my other kids. He played on his high school golf team and was good enough to receive a part scholarship to Jefferson Davis Junior College in Alabama. That was the incentive he needed to start college, and I hope he takes advantage of these years.

I doubt Ricky will turn out to be any Rhodes Scholar but I want him to be exposed to college life and education. There will be time enough for him to start a career after college, even in golf.

He's very conscious of my having money. One summer he didn't want to get a job and asked me to send him money for golf and gambling. "Oh, yeah," I said. "I remember how I had someone supporting me when I was your age."

He told me times have changed.

"Times may have changed," I said, "but people haven't. You're going to have to work your way through the ranks like I did."

But he's a nice young man. He's witty and he smiles and laughs like I do. You can tell he's mine.

I think he might have a chance to make it playing golf, although he hasn't done anything spectacular yet. He has the determination and guts I have and he doesn't mind sweating and practicing. I've seen him hit 1,500 balls a day and he couldn't understand why he was shooting 77 or 78 when he was practicing that hard. I just told him it takes more time.

You never know. You might see another Trevino out there someday.

Clyde has done a tremendous job in raising Lesley, Tony and Troy when I've been away from home so much. They're good kids and we always have great times when we're together.

Lesley wants to be a lot of things. She wants to be a veterinarian and has picked up every stray animal in the neighborhood since she was a baby. She loves to play the piano and wants to teach piano. She loves ballet and has danced with the Dallas Ballet in *The Nutcracker,* but I don't think she'll ever be a ballerina. She's a beautiful girl but she has my bone structure. She's not the tall, wiry type of ballerina you usually see.

She should have been a broom. She can sweep you off your feet. She really does want to be an actress and maybe she will be. If she acts on the screen like she does around the house, trying to snow old Dad, she'll win an Academy Award the first year.

She's not shy. She did her first television commercial when she was sixteen, working with me on one for Bridgestone tires. She had dialogue, so it paid extremely well, enough to cover her expenses for college and then some.

I doubt we'll ever see Lesley try professional golf. As for Tony and Troy, it's too early to say.

Tony has played in the *Dallas Times Herald* junior tournament and some events at Royal Oaks Country Club like the father-son tournament, but he only has a casual interest in golf. That's good. He likes other sports, particularly soccer, and I haven't pushed him.

I've seen boys play so much golf in their early years that they got tired of it. Then when they got to high school age they discarded it because it took time they wanted to spend running around with girls. I want to do just the opposite with Tony, where he can see a lot of improvement when he's sixteen or so and maybe won't burn out.

Troy likes golf and she has her own little clubs, so she can go out and hit some balls when I'm practicing. I'm not predicting we have another Nancy Lopez, however.

She usually won't hit very many. Then she plays on the

grass or sits and watches me. She tends to like golf because she wants to be with me. If her father was digging a ditch or mowing the lawn she would want to be there, too. And that's one of the nicest compliments I've ever had.

So much changed around Dallas through the years, but I always knew I could go by and see Hardy Greenwood at the driving range. But one September morning in 1980 I knew I was going for the last time.

Hardy learned that June that he was losing his lease. W. W. Caruth, Jr., the son of the man I caddied for as a kid, always treated Hardy as a friend rather than a tenant because he liked Hardy and the driving range just the way his father had. But he came by one day and told Hardy his $600-a-month lease wouldn't be renewed. He finally had an offer too good to refuse. The Caruth estate got $5 million from a company that said it wanted to put a few dozen more apartment houses on the land. Hardy sold his last $2 bucket of balls on Labor Day, then closed the business.

He had a party for some of the old-timers at the range the next day, and I flew home from New York for it. I could have stayed up East and made more money playing exhibitions for a couple of days but I knew there would be a lot more exhibitions. There was only one party at Hardy's.

It was a shame to see the driving range disappear like that, just like it was to see the par-3 course next to the range wiped out back in 1970 to make room for the Old Town shopping center. I guess everything has to come to an end, and Hardy was getting a little too old for that busy schedule at the range. Almost everybody had been by there to hit some balls at one time or another, even Bob Hope.

Hardy's wife, Gray, had died from leukemia a few years earlier, and maybe it was time for him to slow down. He'd always been a worker, though, so I set him up with a golf repair shop in Inwood Village. That gave him something to do, but not too much.

The morning of the party we started drinking beer at ten and hitting balls. Hardy, who's just a little taller than I am, was out there dressed as usual, wearing one of my caps and shirts with the sombrero emblem on them, his steel-rim glasses glistening in the sun. I thought about the first time I met him when I was eight, and all the years I played there and worked there, and our arguments, which never were bigger than our friendship. I thought about selling Christmas trees and building the par-3 course.

Then I thought of something else. I needed a beer.

Hardy was enjoying himself, celebrating the end of twenty-five good years. I was glad I was part of them. He was as much a father as anyone I ever had. I absolutely adore the man. He has a son and a daughter, but I think he cares as much for me as he does for his own children. That's why he always felt so strongly about what I did with my life.

He wanted to see me become a great golfer and I think he always knew deep down I was going to make it. But he knew I had to find my own way. What he did with me may have been a toughening process. He didn't want me to have everything easy, and I know I'm better today because I didn't.

Hardy turned it around for me. He taught me that in any walk of life you can achieve two things: honesty and integrity. If you don't have those, you don't have anything. I'm lucky he was on my side.

We hit balls for a while that morning, then settled down to some serious beer drinking and gambling. There must have been a dozen of us jammed in that old shack and we were playing cards on the table, counter and floor. There was a lot of laughing and cussing going on, depending on who was winning at the time, and pretty soon the trash barrel was overflowing with empty beer cans.

Someone yelled we were out of beer, so I darted through the traffic on Lovers Lane to a store and brought back two more cases of Coors. I made quite a few more trips and I'll bet the people in those apartment houses wondered what all those honking horns and screeching tires were about.

Clyde called me at three. The party was still roaring. "Are you going to pick up the kids?" she asked me. "The what?" I said. "Oh, forget it," she said, and hung up. Hell, we were just getting started.

I had $300 in my pocket when I got there and nothing when I woke up the next morning. I guess what I didn't lose on cards I spent on beer, but we had one great time. I don't know how late I was there or how I got home. I won't drive when I've been drinking a lot, so somebody must have driven me home and helped me get in the house.

I know it would be dramatic to say I went back out and hit one last ball into the sunset that day, but the party was going too good for that. Besides, at Hardy's the tees faced north.

And before I drank too much beer I made one important deal with Hardy. I bought 6,000 range balls.

You see, he also taught me there's a fortune in old golf balls. If I were offered my choice of running the bar or the driving range at a club I'd take the range every time. You sell a bottle of whiskey once and it's gone, but those balls are like prostitutes. You never know how much they've been used.

When I was inducted into the World Golf Hall of Fame in September of 1981 I passed another milestone. Now I know that someday I can officially become a has-been. And I'd much rather be a has-been than a never-was.

It means that when I'm sixty-two and sitting at the bar and I meet some guy who never saw me play, he may ask me, "How good were you?" "Well," I'll tell him, "I'm in the Hall of Fame."

It's a rare honor, one that means so much to me that I passed up $50,000 appearance money at the Bob Hope Classic in England to go to Pinehurst, North Carolina, for my induction. I was voted in by the media, and if the media think you belong there, then you must have been pretty good.

A great many golfers, football players and baseball players never will get into their Hall of Fame, guys who contributed a tremendous amount to their sport. When I look back on my U.S. Open, British Open and PGA championships and about three dozen other tournaments I've won around the world, the perfect topping is the Hall of Fame.

I just wish it was in a better location. It's great to have a Hall of Fame, but someone sold somebody a bill of goods to put it in Pinehurst. It disturbs me that millions and millions of people will never see it there.

North Carolina is a great golfing state and has some great courses, but Pinehurst is too remote and too hard to reach. I think the Hall of Fame should have been in a big city—Chicago, Dallas, Philadelphia or New York. But wherever it is, it's really gratifying to be part of it.

A lot of people were disturbed that I wasn't elected earlier, once I had become eligible by playing the tour for ten years, but it didn't bother me. I thought there were more deserving players who should have made it before I did.

Billy Casper was as great a player as any of us but he was overlooked simply because he was at his peak during the Jack Nicklaus–Gary Player–Arnold Palmer era in the 1960s. He won a lot of big tournaments but he never received the attention he deserved. He was elected a year before I was.

I was honored to have Gary Player induct me because we have become very close through the years. He came from a tough background, too. If he hadn't worked his way to the top as a world-class golfer he might have spent his life in the mines in South Africa.

I told him once, "I'm very lucky. If it wasn't for golf I don't know what I'd be doing."

"What do you mean?" he asked me.

"If my IQ had been two points lower," I said, "I'd have been a plant somewhere."

Well, he thought that was so funny he opened my induction with it. Gary knows me so well that he can stand up and say anything about me and it won't bother me. And, what the hell, it got a big laugh.

Life is beautiful. Unfortunately, there's not enough of it. All of a sudden I wake up in the morning and I'm going on forty-three years old and I can remember things I did when I was seventeen like it was yesterday. I look in the mirror and I don't see the wrinkles. I don't see the gray hair. I don't feel as old as I am.

But then I look at someone else my age and I say, "Goddamn, he looks old!" That mirror lies like hell. It's funny how you can't see yourself old, or heavy. But it's there.

I guess the way the Lord tells you you're getting old is that you don't jump out of bed in the morning like you used to. Once I could wake up, grab a driver and hit the ball 250 yards down the middle of the fairway. Now I have to hit at least fifty balls and do some stretching exercises before I try that.

But my life's still fun and I'm glad so many of these things were meant to happen to me. I love my wife, I love my children, and I love my friends. I'm happy that I've made the money I have playing a game and seeing the world along the way. It's a good life and I'm looking forward to more.

In my acceptance speech at Pinehurst I said, "When you play a sport you have two things in mind. One is to get into the Hall of Fame and the other is to go to Heaven when you die." I looked up to the sky and said, "I hope He doesn't need me up there any time soon."

ABOUT THE AUTHOR

Sam Blair, who wrote this book with Lee
Trevino, is a native of Dallas and grew up near
Tenison Park, where Trevino enjoyed some of his
early golfing success. A writer and a columnist
for the Dallas *Morning News*, Blair has won
more than a dozen awards in the Golf Writers
Association of America competition, as well as a
variety of national and state awards for his
writing on major sports. He has written four
other books, including *Staubach*, *First Down*,
Lifetime to Go (with Bob St. John) and *Earl
Campbell: The Driving Force*.